Healing Justice

Healing Justice

Holistic Self-Care for Change Makers

LORETTA PYLES

OXFORD
UNIVERSITY PRESS

OXFORD
UNIVERSITY PRESS

Oxford University Press is a department of the University of Oxford. It furthers
the University's objective of excellence in research, scholarship, and education
by publishing worldwide. Oxford is a registered trade mark of Oxford University
Press in the UK and certain other countries.

Published in the United States of America by Oxford University Press
198 Madison Avenue, New York, NY 10016, United States of America.

Library of Congress Cataloging-in-Publication Data
Names: Pyles, Loretta, author.
Title: Healing justice : holistic self-care for change makers / Loretta Pyles.
Description: New York : Oxford University Press, [2018] |
Includes bibliographical references and index.
Identifiers: LCCN 2017036635 (print) | LCCN 2017040788 (ebook) |
ISBN 9780190663094 (updf) | ISBN 9780190663100 (epub) |
ISBN 9780190663087 (alk. paper)
Subjects: LCSH: Mind and body. | Holistic education. | Social action.
Classification: LCC BF151 (ebook) | LCC BF151 .P95 2018 (print) |
DDC 158—dc23
LC record available at https://lccn.loc.gov/2017036635

For Dora and Silvio

Contents

PART II: *Holistic Self-Care Practices and Skills*

Acknowledgments

THIS BOOK HAS BEEN a culmination of my life's work up to this point, a tremendous opportunity for growth, and a real labor of love. I am sincerely grateful for all the support, feedback, and inspiration I have received during the writing of it. While this writing was a solo journey, community clearly played a fundamental role not only in the intersubjective understandings that I have attempted to articulate here but also through the direct and indirect support of fellow sojourners, family, and friends.

I am very grateful for the feedback that I received from Dana Bliss, Maia Duerr, Carol Horton, and additional blind reviewers. It has truly deepened and strengthened this work. I also have to acknowledge the countless thinkers, writers, activists, spiritual teachers, and cyber "friends" who have helped me to formulate and clarify some of these ideas. Thanks to Sreyashi Chakravarty for her help with the tedious work of citations and references and to Andrew Dominello and Isaac Priyakumar for their editorial support.

Hugs to Gwendolyn Adam and Shanna Goldman, who continue to offer me tremendous support and inspiration on the path of healing justice. I am grateful to the faculty and staff of the School of Social Welfare at UAlbany for their encouragement and support, with special thanks to Heather Horton and Salome Raheim. I also express gratitude to my MSW and PhD students, yoga students, workshop participants, and trainees who humble me, teach me, and inspire me to teach.

I am especially grateful for the many times that my loving family has listened to my woes or cheered me on—Dawne, Tom ("Skip"), Rachel, Seth, Aaron, Yianna, Dora, and Silvio. I offer a special shout-out to my dear sister-in-law, Melissa ("Lissy"), for her unconditional love and support.

Thanks to Insight Meditation Society where I have found refuge through regular silent retreats that continue to heal me and awaken me to the truths of this world. To all my Kripalu sisters and brothers, "Jai

Bhagwan!" To the mountains, trees, and streams that provided the backdrop for much of the writing, I bow to you. Hugs and snuggles to my furry friends—Alex, Tara, and Joey.

Last but not least, Ted Mehl. What can I say to you but this: "you're the best thing that every happened to me." Thank you for editing, researching, and helping me to think through some of this. I deeply cherish our now almost two decades of discussions about politics, philosophy, and spiritual practice. I won't rehash how obnoxious I have been over these many months, so I'll just say, "I'm sorry" and "thank you."

Introduction

TWENTY YEARS AGO, I was working at a feminist domestic violence program, helping battered women find refuge, and actively engaged in anti-oppressive social practice, endeavoring with others to address issues of violence in relation to gender, race, class, disability, and sexual orientation in our community, our organization, the lives of the women we worked with, and ourselves. Though very challenging, exhausting, and often vexing, it was exciting to be in the trenches doing the day-to-day work of social justice and to be connected to a larger feminist antiviolence movement. This connection gave my work meaning and provided a sense of belonging and identity.

At the same time, I was coping with a difficult intimate relationship that was slowly falling apart, rehearsing the intergenerational challenges of my childhood and culture, and feeling like a broken person. To say I wasn't taking very good care of myself would be an understatement. I was full of grief and despair, I didn't understand who I was, and I couldn't make sense of the world I was living in.

Burned out, I eventually left that work and started to find other ways of understanding and helping the world and myself. Over the course of many years, as I started slowing down, meditating, doing yoga, practicing compassion for myself and others, and engaging in self- and group inquiry, I began to have more experiences of being present and satisfied in my body, genuinely feeling my emotions, having more cohesion between my work life and personal passions, being more successful and impactful in my work, and feeling deeper connections to the people and the world around me. Though I certainly hadn't arrived at some final destination (and most certainly still haven't, and clearly never will, as that is not the point), I was on a *path*, a path of aligning the inner work of healing, self-compassion, and attending to my own suffering and internalized oppression with the outer work of accompanying people, interrupting injustice, and effecting change.

One experience signifies this alignment in my mind and it culminated during a five-day Zen meditation retreat in 2000. At the time, I was working for another antiviolence organization, but this time doing statewide policy advocacy work on behalf of community-based organizations. Unconventional though it was, I received permission to leave the retreat for a few hours because I had an important meeting to attend with my colleagues. The meeting was with the governor's chief of staff to talk about funding for domestic violence programs that would address some of the survivors' economic needs. The governor had proposed unjust cuts to the budget, and we were ready for a fight. Going into the meeting and by that time having been meditating regularly for about a year and, in the case of this retreat, for a couple of days from early morning until night, I felt particularly open, empowered, and clear. I was also able to work with letting go of my expectations about the outcome of the meeting too, which I think freed me up to allow for any possibility. I can't remember or describe exactly what happened in that meeting, but we came away with all of the funding we had originally proposed. Without any struggle, they reversed their decision and reinstated all the funding for survivors of domestic violence into the state budget.

I attribute our success that day to our solidarity and strength over the course of many months through our ongoing work with our own constituents and persistent advocacy with state actors. And yet perhaps something a little magical happened that day too. We knew we were on the side of justice and our presence was formidable. We were able to communicate in a calm yet firm way what the right thing to do was. That moment has always shown me the power of aligning the inner with the outer. Who knows, perhaps if I had walked into that meeting crazy-eyed and burnt out, maybe we would have received the funding too. But the experience piqued my interest in the connection between my meditation work and my social change work. I am not intimating that when you meditate everything is going to go your way, or you'll be able to change what political party is in office, or get your client to stop drinking heavily, or end racism. Rather, I am pointing toward the prospect of what creating a little bit of space in the mind-heart can do, potentially allowing one to move beyond conditioned patterning that can disempower and deplete a person, creating an opening for new possibilities to emerge.

In my work today as a social work educator, researcher, community practitioner, consultant, yoga and meditation teacher, and trainer, it has become clear that some of the practitioners around me—community organizers, therapists, educators, academic colleagues, and my social work students who are working in the field—are suffering. Like myself, their calling in life is to help people, to alleviate injustice, and to effect social change. They are doing this work in public social services agencies, hospitals, clinics, schools, and community-based organizations and in a range of policy settings. Nevertheless, I see chronic exhaustion from overwork in organizations that are grinding people down; corrosive anger toward a patriarchal, racist, and capitalist system; and anxiety and despair over the chipping away at what seems like the last vestiges of a social safety net. My students who are taking classes and working as unpaid interns, all on top of part-time or full-time paid work, are being victimized by an unforgiving system right out of the starting gates of their career.

All of this is happening in a context and culture where many organizations and practitioners do not have the time, privilege, or inclination to inquire into the deeper structural causes of these problems nor discern the ways that these problems impact who they are and how they are functioning. And the fallout and coping behaviors of this scenario can actually be a little bit ugly—petty infighting, workplace bullying, substance abuse, caffeine and technology addiction, and unhealthy eating habits, to name a few, not to mention mediocre job performance. And it's not exactly their fault; given the harsh and underresourced environments, these outcomes are the logical conclusion. Thus, for many of the people I work with, rallying cries for self-care seem like a cruel joke.

And so my vocation has become focused on how to alleviate some of these challenges by bringing healing practices to social workers, activists, and other helping professionals and the organizations and movements that they are a part of, sharing what I have learned from my years of studying and practicing mindfulness and yoga in relation to social change and human services work. While the practices inspired by mindfulness and yoga are not a panacea for all of our problems—neither personal ones nor social ones—my work has come to focus on the ways that these practices can illuminate and sustain the path for those of us who are called to serve. Indeed, I have come to believe, like many others,[1] that this personal work—healing one's body, mind, and relationships—is a necessary part of social work.

My social work students have been saying for many years that their professors and field supervisors are always telling them to practice self-care but that they never teach them *how to actually do it*. And so I began to proactively teach them how to meditate, guiding them in mindful movement and facilitating more opportunities for collective inquiry into and engagement with the social origins of, and embodied impacts of, oppression. In the classroom, this has allowed for more opportunities to identify creative and responsive solutions to injustice and suffering. It was scary at first as I sat there thinking (and still sometimes do), "They are going to hate this;" "I'm going to get fired for this;" and many other troubling thoughts. In spite of the voices in my head, I have persisted. And, it turns out that, by and large, students really love it. In fact, they seem to be hungry for it. I took this kind of work into various communities and started teaching self-care to practitioners, offering practical and impactful mind-body skills as a key, and often overlooked, support of human services, counseling, and community organizing work. Moreover, as an activist and engaged scholar, my colleagues and I began to incorporate healing, soul feeding, and group visioning as a valuable part of building community and social justice seeking. Consequently, this book is the outgrowth of my practice, teaching, and study of what I, and others, have come to think of as healing justice.

Healing Justice

Healing justice is a concept and practice that has slowly been emerging in the past decade in response to a more callous neoliberal context, amplified by global economic policies that continue to empower an elite group of actors, ongoing antagonism to those who are "other," and a culture that encourages people to disconnect from themselves and each other. An increasingly diverse contingent of activists, particularly immigrants and people of color, queer people, and young people, have turned toward that which activists in the past have not necessarily attended to—the impact of violence and intergenerational trauma; the body, emotions, and spirit; and individual and collective practices that can facilitate deeper understanding, connection, and sustainability.

During the 2010 US Social Forum, activists created this working definition of healing justice, describing it as

> a framework that identifies how we can holistically respond to and intervene on generational trauma and violence and bring collective

practices that can impact and transform the consequences of oppression on our bodies, hearts and minds. Through this framework we built two political and philosophical convergences of healing inside of liberation.[2]

Chicago-based organizer Tanuja Jagernaut further notes that healing justice "recognizes that we *have* bodies, minds, emotions, hearts, and it makes the connection that we cannot do this work of transforming society and our communities without bringing collective healing into our work."[3] Healing justice, as I understand it, is a practice of attention and connection, a way of healing a sense of fracturedness or disconnection that may be a result of trauma, oppressive socio-cultural narratives and practices, or the myriad ways in which humans may lose touch with each other and themselves. It is a practice that asks social practitioners of all kinds to cultivate the conditions that might allow them to feel more whole and connected to themselves, the world around them, and other human beings.

Given the unique challenges faced in the world today, where people tend to be very connected to technology, ideologies, and people who are like them and less connected to others who are different from them, the natural world, and the parts of themselves that they reject, the ability to cultivate relationships by tapping into their intuition and collective resilience is as critical as ever and is something that must be reclaimed. In an interview with *YES! Magazine*, social justice activist Angela Davis wrote,

> I think our notions of what counts as radical have changed over time. Self-care and healing and attention to the body and the spiritual dimension—all of this is now a part of radical social justice struggles. That wasn't the case before. And I think that now we're thinking deeply about the connection between interior life and what happens in the social world. Even those who are fighting against state violence often incorporate impulses that are based on state violence in their relations with other people.[4]

And so, healing justice is a practice that asks people to heal each other and themselves, change the way they relate to each other and organize themselves, and continually interrogate their tactics and interventions. This book attempts to offer guidance in such work, for anyone interested in embarking on or continuing a path of healing justice.

Overview of the Book

Each chapter of this book begins with a brief *case study* of an individual or group, which serves as a touchstone throughout the chapter. The case studies are composites based on people I have known in my more than 20 years of experience doing social change and healing justice work. Though the case studies are fabricated, they are inspired by the lives and work of colleagues, students, supervisors, and friends. The organizations are based on those I have worked in myself, consulted or supported, or ones my students worked in. Throughout each chapter, I present what I hope are engaging and useful ideas and concepts related to the topic, along with extensive social and cultural analysis. This discussion serves to help readers to deconstruct the stories, values, institutions, and policies that contribute to the need for and sidetrack us from healing justice work.

Throughout the chapter, when appropriate, I give attention to research studies on the issues and the intervention evidence base on the holistic self-care interventions offered. As the research evidence is still new and has many shortcomings, I critique this literature, identifying gaps, as well as the ways that such scientific inquiry may sometimes be at odds with a healing justice agenda. To illuminate the topic more comprehensively and impactfully, I attend to other ways of knowing, such as practice wisdom (my own and others) and the insights from contemplative mind-body practices, particularly modern Buddhism, modern postural yoga, and contemporary Ayurveda, which are my root holistic self-care practices.[5] The chapters stay focused on the transformative vision of this book, emphasizing that self-care and healing justice are ultimately for social change, serving as an antidote to the growing body of literature on self-care that may arguably perpetuate neoliberal narcissism, ignorance of social privilege, cultural appropriation, and a fatalism regarding oppressive social systems. The last part of each chapter is focused on *putting it into practice*, specifically offering a personal *inquiry*, a new self-care *skill* to learn, and an *experiment* to try for a day, aiding readers in cultivating and deepening their knowledge, values, and skills related to the chapter topic.

Part I begins with Chapter 1, where I frame healing justice as a response to a far-reaching social field that produces oppression and trauma. I continue by articulating healing justice within a broader concept of transformative social practice, whereby community work and social change are done in ways that decolonize, pay attention to process, and tend to internalized oppression. In Chapter 2, I focus on the need for self-care as it relates to stress and stress reduction, a need that has arisen out of the global economic conditions, the frantic monetized digital environment, and inequitable social systems and relations. I also discuss and analyze current research on self-care practice and begin to introduce some of the holistic practices that are central to the book. In Chapter 3, I explain the meaning of the term "whole self," moving from a discussion of the mind-body connection to the idea of an ecological self, expanding the discussion to include connections to community, nature, and spirit. I articulate some basic ideas from the Buddhist and yogic traditions that animate the practices taught in the book, noting how these traditions have been adapted and Westernized in numerous ways. It is in this chapter that I introduce a visual representation of the healing justice framework. Chapter 4 picks up on the capabilities necessary for healing justice– mindfulness, compassion, curiosity, critical inquiry, equanimity, and effort. I explain their roots in contemplative practices, mind-body medicine, and neuroscience and their relevance to healing justice.

In Part II, "Holistic Self-Care Practices and Skills," readers are introduced to inquiries, research, practices, and skill development geared around key dimensions of the whole self. Chapter 5 introduces the indigenous medicine of India, known as Ayurveda, which acknowledges the changing conditions and diverse constitutions of everyone, thus contradicting homogenizing solutions to self-care that saturate the marketplace. The chapter focuses on the body, breaking down self-care into three key domains—eating, moving, and resting. Chapter 6 is concerned with the mind-heart, bringing attention to both the emotional and cognitive aspects of the self, offering new skills for working with the emotions and attending to beliefs so that practitioners can be more empowered in their endeavors. In Chapter 7, drawing from the ways that activists have historically and currently sustain themselves with spirituality and religion, the chapter focuses on connecting with spirit. The chapter introduces self-care practices appropriate for all spiritual traditions while also attending to the ways that religions have marginalized people through discrimination, spiritual abuse, and cultural appropriation.

Chapter 8 is concerned with the communal dimension of the self and is exemplified through discussion of human tendencies toward collectivism, cooperation, and altruism, notwithstanding the pervasiveness of Western individualism. The chapter explores ideas such as empathy and community resilience and offers healing justice practices to do with others as a community. Chapter 9 concludes this section by inviting readers to reclaim their connections to the natural or nonhuman world as a form of healing. Each chapter continues with social analysis on the dimension of the self in question, continuing to introduce holistic practices grounded in East-West teachings, meaning Buddhist, yogic, and Ayurvedic practices that originated in Eastern contexts and were adapted to a Western context. The chapters are especially focused on introducing specific practices and exercises with instructions for readers to engage in them alone and/or with others.

In Part III, "Where the Rubber Hits the Road," readers connect the theoretical framework of Part I, with the whole self practices of Part II, with the goal of engaging in healing justice work in practice contexts on the front lines. Specifically, Chapter 10 is concerned with ways practitioners can cultivate healing justice organizations that support transformative self-care for workers and clients alike. Analyzing the literature on burnout, I discuss issues such as employee workload, transparency in decision-making, worker control, and quality supervision and review several organizational models/types that serve as prototypes for healing justice organizations. In Chapter 11, attention shifts to ways that healing justice practices can be applied in one's direct practice with individuals, groups, and communities, including issues to think about when sharing the practices with others, including clients, who have limited access to wellness. Chapter 12 takes a wider lens focusing on how to cultivate a global empathic consciousness and to bring the wisdom of healing justice to global social change efforts. This chapter also serves as a conclusion to the whole book, offering opportunities to reflect on one's self, the global community, and one's vocation going forward.

Sanskrit and Pali words are generally italicized in the text. All diacritics have been omitted for ease of readability. Common usage terms such as yoga are not italicized.

Healing Justice

PART I

*Healing Justice and
Whole Self-Care*

I

Oppression, Trauma, and Healing Justice

"If you have come here to help me, you are wasting your time. But if you have come because your liberation is bound up with mine, then let us work together."
—LILA WATSON, Australian Aboriginal Activist

Case Study

The Asian Women's Health Project (AWHP) was started in 1986 and grew out of a fundamental concern for the health and safety of women in a patriarchal culture that condones domination of their lives and precludes access to healthcare and reproductive justice. While Asian and Pacific Islander women come from diverse cultural backgrounds, they are united in the barriers that they face to health and reproductive healthcare—lack of bilingual and bicultural providers, limited knowledge of the healthcare system, inadequate insurance coverage, and challenges with transportation and childcare. AWHP's work focuses on offering services to women, resources and capacity building to providers, as well as organizing and advocacy to effect changes in the healthcare system. Several years ago, they also began to realize that there was a need for increasing access to traditional Asian health remedies (e.g. herbs, acupuncture, and mind-body practices), and they have been engaging in education and advocacy efforts toward this end.

AWHP has experienced many changes over the years including the growing pains associated with expanding their offerings and capacities, followed by significant cutbacks in funding and the reality of having to do more with less. Now, a new generation of advocates at the AWHP has begun to question some of the assumptions and decisions of their founding sisters' work. Their questions have revealed tensions in the organization, resulting in stress and a sense of confusion.

Some of this tension is built around resentment toward the government grant-getting activity and the time it has taken away from and perhaps co-opted them from doing the real work and engaging in social change. The younger advocates also want a life for themselves outside of their work—to have a social life and healthy families, pursue outside interests, and contribute to their communities in other ways. Part of the job of staff at AWHP is to support women who are experiencing the ongoing impacts of racism and discrimination, and yet there is no time to attend to their own pain from racism and discrimination. Moreover, with the constant barrage of information to manage, there is clearly a sense of collective burnout as there has been an increase in staff turnover in recent years.

The staff and board of AWHP all agreed that they needed to set aside some time to attend to these issues that have been creeping into their work and to envision what a new way forward might be like. They scheduled a weekend retreat with a facilitator who was tuned into the idea of healing justice and created a weekend for them that would allow for individual and group healing, discussion, and skill building. They began the weekend by telling their stories to one another— the stories of their culture, families, immigration, and assimilation, as well as how the work became important to them. They learned about what each other held dear as well as what they had lost. They continued the retreat by talking about what health means to them, drawing a giant visual mandala of wellness that included social health, spiritual health, and the sense of well-being that comes through connection with nature. The weekend was punctuated with movement and dance practices from various Asian traditions, which helped the women to feel more embodied and appreciative of each other's cultures.

All of this paved the wave for more authentic and considered conversations about the issues they were facing, including critical interrogation into the larger economic and funding climate; this resulted in greater empathy for the choices that the founding sisters had felt forced to make over the years. The conversations also centered around healing and self-care, and the group agreed that creating space to reclaim their own traditional healing practices within the context of their day-to-day work was an obvious next step toward healing justice in their lives and work. While they certainly did not solve every problem that weekend, the members of the group found some collective healing and were able to begin to articulate ways forward and identify needed skills that would allow them to support one another in their own individual healing journeys, address intergenerational challenges, navigate the neoliberal climate, and cultivate a sense of wholeness as an organization.

Oppression and Trauma

The social forces of oppression impact people's lives from the moment they come into the world. The realities of systemic oppression, from racism to classism to heterosexism, manifest in endless ways, as it is built on a fundamentally fatal falsehood that people have a right to dominate others. Many social justice thinkers have noted that this delusion harms people both when they are the victims of oppression and when they are the beneficiaries of oppression.[1,2] It leaves its traces in all aspects of the bio-psycho-social-spiritual person and is perpetuated in families, communities, and social institutions.

Oppressive systems, including white supremacist patriarchy, condone the perpetration of physical, emotional, sexual, and spiritual violence and indeed rely on it for their existence, leaving people vulnerable, traumatized, and less powerful in terms of their ability to thrive and to effect change. Whether it is violence in communities, institutions, war zones, or intimate partnerships, the impact of violence is traumatic, if not life threatening. People who are victims of trauma and complex trauma may experience a cycle of hyperarousal and dissociative numbing, anxiety, sleeplessness, chronic pain, and intrusive memories.[3-5] Moreover, "habitual hyper-vigilance, aggression, distrust, and appeasement often result from traumatic experiences" and can play themselves out in movement building and organizational contexts, thus limiting people's sense of agency and a group's collective efficacy.[6]

Trauma may be a result of experiences in one's family of origin that have been perpetuated through many generations. It may also be a result of state violence from war, genocide, and penalization, or through a collectively traumatic experience such as a disaster. Or it may be combinations of these as indigenous families, for example, internalize the violence of colonization through generations of substance abuse. Researchers have identified what they call "adverse childhood experiences" as stressful or traumatic events, such as abuse, which can result in a range of health problems over the life course.[7] Neuroscience and other disciplines are teaching that this trauma, or ACES, can stay in the body and can even be epigenetically transmitted to future generations.[8,9]

In the case of people living with few resources, the constant physical and mental stressors of poverty have been shown to impact the immune system, levels of depression, and other health indicators.[10,11] There is similar research on the impacts of racism.[12] Author Ta-Nehisi Coates[13] has noted the centuries of assault on black bodies—slavery, segregation, and mass incarceration—describing the ways in which it has impacted him, his family, friends, and the community around him. In this era of late capitalism, where profits for elites are growing at the same time economic disparity and environmental devastation are increasing, the need for attention to and the dismantling of these interlocking, intersectional, and intergenerational oppressions is dire.

When studying oppression, whether from a social systemic perspective (macropolitical) or an internalized mind-body or interpersonal perspective (micropolitical), it is essential to inquire into and highlight human strengths, resilience, and resistance. Resilience, which is discussed further in the next chapter, is the capacity and process of adapting to stress and adversity while maintaining physical and psychological functioning.[14] Coates describes beautifully such resilience as evidenced by the literary, artistic, and scientific achievements of African Americans. About himself, he writes:

> The pursuit of knowing was freedom to me, the right to declare your own curiosities and follow them through all manner of books. I was made for the library, not the classroom. The classroom was a jail of other people's interests. The library was open, unending, free.[15]

Despite the trauma of violence, poverty, and racism, human resilience emboldens people to continually create inspiring communities and culture; resist the forces of oppression through protest, organizing, and advocacy; and take care of one another.

More subtle forms of oppression can become internalized as well. For example, women are inundated with messages from the wider culture about having their bodies look a certain way as their bodies are surveilled as objects of the patriarchal gaze, resulting in a painful struggle for many women as they police themselves in order to conform and morph into a certain body image. Women of color will likely experience this in unique and perhaps exacerbated ways compared to those whose body types are more normalized, thus reminding us that oppressions can be interlocking and intersectional, just as the Asian women at AWHP understood.[16] Toni Morrison, author of the novel *The Bluest Eye*, expresses how internalized oppression develops in a young African American girl: "Long hours she sat looking in the mirror, trying to discover the secret of her ugliness, the ugliness that made her ignored or despised at school, by teachers and classmates alike."[17] This kind of internalized oppression, which is often pathologized by a medical model, may manifest as low self-esteem, eating disorders, or problems with drugs or alcohol. A healing justice approach invites practitioners to bring their attention, care, and innate healing capacities to the ways that such oppression manifests in bodies, minds, and spirits.

For men, the message that sharing one's feelings or vulnerability makes them "less than a man" most certainly impacts their thoughts and actions. And for those men who are from historically marginalized communities, there will also be a differential experience with this phenomenon. Further, for those who may not identify within this binary gender framework, the positive messages and images that queer, nonconforming, and transgender people receive are few and far between, as the lack of recognition and hatred of society can reach deep into the body and psyche, resulting in self-hatred and self-destructive patterning, compounded by a lack of access to support services to alleviate this suffering.[18] Hence these disempowering discourses and practices that are born out of the dominant culture can, in effect, function to cultivate particular habits of mind and body[19] creating neural pathways that are deeply embedded in the brain.[20] Moreover, they can perpetuate human services work that reinforces the same old social patterns.

Fortunately, humans have the capability to create new patterning in their minds and generate new cultural stories and behaviors that can lead them to a different way of being with themselves and each other. This kind of transformative work can happen alongside one's work to change systems; indeed, in some cases, it is the work itself. I think a powerful example of this is the way that queer activists have embraced self-care and mutual aid as part of the struggle itself. After the Orlando, Florida, massacre at a nightclub full of lesbian, gay, bisexual, transgender, and queer people, queer people posted the hashtag #queerselflove, reminding each other and the world that loving themselves just as they are is a form of resistance. As transgender writer Kate Bornstein said about queer activism, "Do whatever it takes to make your life more worth living. . . . Just don't be mean."[21] This insight perhaps points to compassion and self-compassion as vital elements of healing justice work.

Also worthy of acknowledging and understanding is how privileged people experience suffering within the confines of a hegemonic social system despite benefitting from it in innumerable ways. For example, being obsessed with money or image can fuel anxiety disorders, obsessive-compulsive disorders, and depression. Additionally, many white people may find themselves feeling a range of difficult emotions or states when confronted with the realities of racism—from defensiveness to guilt or shame to paralysis. Indeed, the whole gamut of these experiences, arising from oppressive social frameworks and practices, I argue, is also worthy of our attention, care, and compassion and essential to healing. When people with privilege are able to work through some of their initial resistance, or what has been called "white fragility,"[22] there is more opportunity to go deeply into the undoing of white supremacy.

Moreover, the secondary or vicarious trauma of helpers working in community-based contexts can produce some of the exact same symptoms as someone experiencing direct trauma.[23] Practitioners who are working on the front lines of these issues—from social workers in child welfare agencies to indigenous activists protesting tar sands extraction to #BlackLivesMatter activists resisting police violence—are often grappling with a toxic combination of external and internalized oppression; personal, familial, and community trauma; and secondary trauma and burnout. In addition, the stress of making ends meet in an economy that is not favorable to people working in nonprofits adds to this burden. Black queer Buddhist meditation teacher angel kyodo Williams, writes:

> For, until our capital-V vision for liberation gives way to an accessible, translatable, adaptable yet rigorous praxis at meaningful scale—one that can match in energy and rebound through rhythm from the sustained stress the structures of oppression are designed to burden our minds, our bodies, and our hearts with—we cannot uproot these forces.[24]

Indeed, practitioners need a way of doing their social practice that is sustainable and continually invites them to reconnect with themselves, each other, and the natural world around them. Fortunately, research on activists is showing that mind-body practices can help them to bolster their resilience, transform trauma, foster alliances in organizations, and prepare them for the rigors of direct action.[25] The same is true for counselors and other helping professionals, namely, that when practitioners and practitioners-in-training have an opportunity to learn and practice self-care and other healing justice skills, there is, at the very least, less burnout and more possibility for empathy, connection, and efficacy.[26]

Introducing Healing Justice

In recent years, activists who have been concerned with the connections to be made among oppression, trauma, burnout, self-care, and collective healing have proposed the idea of *healing justice* as an antidote and critical dimension of transformative social practice. Taking a lead from black feminist poet Audre Lorde, who famously said, "Caring for myself is not self-indulgence, it is self-preservation, and that is an act of political warfare," a new generation of practitioners is devoting time, energy, and resources to this kind of healing work. For example, a group known as Kindred, a healing justice collective located in the southern United States, affirms that healing justice is needed to

> be able to respond to the increased state of burnout and depression in our movements; systematic loss of our communities' healing traditions; the isolation and stigmatization of healers, and the increased privatization of our land, medicine and natural resources that has caused us to rely on state or private models we do not trust and that do not serve us.[27]

These groups are made up of diverse actors who identify as activists, social practitioners, healers, and mind-body workers.

Healing justice is both a paradigm and a set of practices that invites practitioners to heal themselves at the same time that they heal the world. It is a response to the intergenerational trauma that has accumulated in the mind-body continuum that is today calling for compassionate and wise attention. According to Berila, "Since oppression creates deep trauma, it only makes sense that disrupting oppression and healing from it will require more than political and intellectual processes; it will also require embodied ones."[28] As I conceive it, it is a practice done with and on behalf of the whole self, which includes the body, mind, heart, spirit, community, and natural world.

People who are living and teaching holistic practices such as mindfulness and yoga,[29] and who are concerned with what has been termed "a well-being gap" or "wellness gap,"[30] inspire another entrée into this work on healing justice. To be sure, this conversation should be considered within the larger question of who has access to quality healthcare, including complementary health treatments, which is currently a critical conversation in the United States and elsewhere. The well-being gap is a divide that exists "between who gets to be well and who doesn't."[31] It is acknowledgment of the fact that people with privilege have access to wellness (healthcare, alternative treatments, time for meditation, money for yoga and exercise classes, and access to organic healthy food) while so many others do not.

Unmistakably, there is an important argument to be made that a fixation on personal wellness distracts many activists and would-be activists from dismantling oppressive systems and pursuing social justice more robustly, as they instead remain self-involved with green smoothies and Pilates. To be sure, yoga has become a transnational commodity, yet another product for sale in a consumer culture.[32] Both mindfulness and modern postural yoga have developed in a Western context and have arguably embraced the individualist values of the Enlightenment, contemporary fitness paradigms (in the case of yoga), and worldviews grounded in modern psychology and metaphysics.[33] Thus one key area of inquiry in this book going forward concerns to what extent mindfulness and yoga could be perpetuating the problems of individualism, isolation, and divides between haves and have-nots.

A group called CTZNWell seeks to counter the potential solipsism of modern mindfulness and yoga practices and maintains that "no one can be well unless everyone is well." In their efforts to reclaim well-being for everyone, this group has worked on the fight for a higher minimum wage, voter registration, and more just food policies. Other groups, such as Off The Mat into the World, are leveraging the strength and insight they have gained from their yoga practice to take action on issues of oppression including poverty, violence, and access to healthcare. The Yoga Service Council is building the capacity of yoga teachers and others to share yoga with people who would not otherwise have access to yoga, including veterans, people who are incarcerated, and people who are differently abled. In the world of mindfulness and modern Western Buddhism, Buddhist Peace Fellowship is a group that seeks "to help beings liberate themselves from the suffering that manifests in individuals, relationships, institutions, and social systems," as they focus on ecological justice, gender justice, and prison justice. Thus healing justice is equally concerned with healing oneself, one's colleagues, and the communities one is a part of as well as supporting the healing of communities that one is not a part of. It is one piece of a larger framework for transformative social practice, which I discuss next.

Transformative Social Practice

Progressive social change movements embrace the idea that oppression is so deeply entrenched and corrosive that a fundamental change in social systems is needed. Climate change activists, queer activists, and radical social workers tend to agree that just creating more inclusivity into and access to an already unjust system is not enough. They are called to transform social, economic, and cultural institutions, discourses, and practices, as they simultaneously work to liberate themselves from the tyranny of this oppression. This kind of transformative practice, which affirms that attention to micropolitics is as important as macropolitics, has its roots in multiple traditions that have grown out of both modern and postmodern eras.[34] Relevant concepts include transformative justice, transformative pedagogy, transformative politics, transformative social work practice, transformative community organizing, and transformative social change.[35]

While the term "transformative" is used in many disciplines, such as women's studies, education, psychology, political science, and social work, it has not been as heavily theorized as one might think. As well, it has sometimes been a term, like "empowerment" or "social justice" (and indeed like "mindfulness" and "yoga") that has been co-opted, watered down, and become arguably empty of meaning. Thus it is vital to continually define it in collaboration with others, embedded in one's particular context. Here I outline what I take to be key dimensions of transformative social practice that have emerged from my experiences and studies as a scholar, teacher, and practitioner working in various settings, distilling some general themes meant to serve as a touchstone for readers. Clarifying transformative social practice will help situate healing justice as one of its critical dimensions.

Transformative social practice is process-oriented social change and healing work that seeks to alter existing political, economic, and social systems while also transforming individuals. It is a pathway to material and spiritual liberation for everyone, including both the human and non-human worlds. Like the Lila Watson quote indicates at the beginning of the chapter, transformative social practice blurs the boundaries between helper and helped and recognizes that our fates are linked. There are several basic premises that underlie transformative practice as I, and others going before me, have conceived it:

1. *There is a synergistic relationship between the personal and the political.* This idea was embraced in second-wave feminist movements and

recognizes that individual experiences of oppression are manifestations of larger social forces. These systems socially reproduce who we are, reflecting the existing order and cementing power for the privileged. Ideas from critical theory, feminist theory, general systems theory, deep ecology, and cognitive science offer further support for this premise about the interrelationship between self and society. In fact, we are often cocreating or reproducing oppressive systems moment to moment. Importantly, the same logic applies to our liberation, namely that we have the capacity to cocreate liberatory practices and spaces.

2. *We must work to change the structures and operations of historically oppressive social systems.* Social change is not inevitable, nor is fatalism an option. Transformative practice requires us to do the challenging work of changing political processes, governmental policies and institutions, schools and institutions of higher education, and organizations of all kinds, including for-profit, nonprofit, and public. This vision also invites us to take the risks of creating new and alternative ways of organizing ourselves in terms of economic activities, the environment, education, social services, and intimate relations.

3. *Moment to moment, we endeavor to decolonize the spaces in which we work, live, and take care of ourselves.* This means that we honestly look at the ways that racism, Eurocentrism, Islamophobia, classism, sexism, homophobia, gender tyranny, transphobia, ableism, fat phobia, and every form of colonization of "the other" manifests in our thoughts, words, and deeds. This requires authentic participation in critical conversations, conducted with as much humility and love as we are able. Moreover, we endeavor to meet each other where we are. It asks us to be willing to be with a wide range of our own and others' sometimes uncomfortable emotions and ideas. We also seek to decolonize the spaces where we care for ourselves, attending to issues of cultural appropriation, cultural humility, and inclusion.

4. *Attending to means and process is vital to our collective liberation.* Living in a neoliberal order that is placing increasing value on outcomes, performance measures, and the bottom line, we have seen the ways that transactional practices where "the ends justify the means" have hurt both the people we work with and ourselves as workers. When we attend to process, we are better able to hear and see one another, bring our whole selves to our work, and critically analyze ideas and the consequences of our actions. We also must recognize that there are sometimes limits in our ability and need to attend to process.

5. *Oppression has a negative impact on our bodies, minds, and spirits.*
Oppression affects not only our minds but also our bodies and spirits.
Because bodies, emotions, and spirit are marginalized in the dominant
patriarchal culture in service to cognition, we must bring extra attention
to these areas and the ways that internalized oppression and trauma
impact these dimensions of ourselves. It is through careful attention to
and celebration of these dimensions of ourselves that we can find our
liberation.

6. *Personal and collective practices of inquiry, care, and healing are necessary
for both sustainability and transformation.* In order to transform oppressive systems, we must heal ourselves. This means we bring compassionate understanding to our communities, families, and ourselves,
as we deepen our relationships. We learn about our conditioning and
our strengths and orient toward our personal and collective growth and
transformation. We can do so both privately and in community, using
methods that resonate with our personal intuition, as well as our culture and communities of birth and/or choice. Healing justice practices
also help us to sustain ourselves and the organizations in which we
work, preventing burnout and promoting wholeness and wellness.

Transformative social practice is manifesting in the work of countless
groups and individuals across around the world. The case study of the
AWHP highlighted the ways that the women were making connections
between their larger agenda related to Asian women's health and the reclamation of their own cultural healing practices for their own well-being.
Another example is indigenous climate change activists in the Pacific
Northwest who are drawing from the wisdom of their spiritual traditions
and using creative direct-action methods like drumming and chanting to
bring attention to the perils of climate change. In the Occupy Wall Street
encampments, activists modeled the kind of world they wanted to live in
by using foot-pedaled power and consensus decision-making. Leaders in
the National Domestic Workers Alliance, who represent nannies, house-
keepers, and caregivers, are incorporating mind-body practices into their
political and grassroots education, including Aikido and generative somat-
ics.[36] Moreover, social service organizations are using the Sanctuary model
to create organizational climates that are trauma sensitive and nonviolent
and that prioritize self-care for both workers and clients.[37]

Transformative social practice is clearly distinctive from conventional ways of engaging in social practice. Examples of the latter include

Alinsky-style organizing that emphasizes "our" victories over "them," social services organizations that are modeled on modern corporations, or clinical practice that focuses only on the alleviation of symptoms. And this is not to say that these endeavors do not have a place or do not help people. But this privileging of efficiency and outcomes turns our attention away from our whole selves, our interconnectedness, the origins of personal and social problems, and the opportunities that this awareness can create for healing. Furthermore, conventional social practice tends to succumb to the fallacy of self-denial in terms of practitioner self-care, often burning workers out, perpetuating trauma, and creating commodified organizational cultures.

To Care or Not to Care

Social problems transpire within human constructed systems and contexts. Practitioners are all simultaneously cocreating and being affected by the systems, institutions, organizations, and communities in which they work and live. As such, they are in need of some degree of the attention, care, and healing that the people and systems they are working with need. To ignore this simple fact, that is, to deny the importance and practice of self-care, is to commit what I call *the fallacy of self-denial.* The fallacy is rooted in a range of conscious and unconscious messages that many people, particularly social change agents and human service workers, have internalized—"There is no time," "I'm too busy," "I feel guilty," "Their problems are worse than mine," "I'm a caregiver, I give to others, that's just who I am," "I maintain boundaries; I don't let my own stuff spill over," "I've worked through my stuff," "Self-care is for those who are weak and I am strong," "My people don't do self-care," "Self-care is for the privileged," "I don't need fixing, it's the system that needs fixing," "I'll start taking care of myself [on some future date]," ad infinitum. To deconstruct the many shades of this harmful fallacy requires practitioners to hold paradox and question stories whose veracity they may have taken for granted, all while continuing to work for change in their communities.

Social change activists, social workers, and helping professionals have complex if not ambivalent relationships to the idea and practice of self-care. To alleviate despair, occupational stress, burnout, secondary or vicarious trauma, grief, and anxiety, human services professionals and other social change agents have lauded the virtues of self-care and resilience building. However, the extent to which self-care is actually taught and modeled in practitioner training programs and in practice contexts has been highly contested.[38] Ben Shepard, for example, wrote about the grief and secondary trauma experienced by staff working with HIV patients in harm reduction programs.[39] He advocates for social services organizations to reimagine and implement a culture of wellness with attention to the role that supervision, support, and peer mentoring can play in changing the culture. He notes, importantly, though, the powerful structural barriers that exist, particularly the fragile funding sources that result in overworked and underpaid staff. For those working in health and treatment settings, the efficiencies of neoliberal insurance models and demands for evidence-based treatments are creating additional pressures and dissonances. Clearly, the structural conditions and context of human services and social change work play an enormous role in manufacturing the fallacy of self-denial.

Despite a substantial body of evidence that self-care can alleviate work-related stress in a variety of social services settings[40] and that resourcing social work and counseling students with self-care tools can bolster their resilience in their internships and future practice settings,[41] there is clearly ambivalence from key gatekeepers in both the helping professions and in social movements. For example, the US National Association of Social Workers issued a policy statement arguing that "professional self-care is an essential component in competent, compassionate, and ethical social work practice, requiring time, energy, and commitment."[42] The American Counseling Association has proffered similar statements in terms of worker ethics and educational policies.[43] However, the US Council on Social Work Education has failed to make professional self-care a requirement in its educational standards.[44] In many social practice settings, the sad reality is that the attitude of managers and others with power in organizations toward self-care is often complete silence on the issue, rhetoric without action, or meager self-care offerings in an organizational context of business as usual.

It is important to remember that the fallacy of self-denial is historically embedded in human services and advocacy work. Louise Knight writes about Jane Addams, one of the early pioneers of the social work profession, a settlement house movement leader, and a Nobel Prize winner for her antiwar activism:

> Evidently, Jane wanted a career that demanded self-sacrifice, even martyrdom, that close cousin of heroism. Martyrs embraced

suffering as destiny, while heroes passed through suffering on their way to victory; martyrs consistently denied the self, while heroes celebrated it; martyrs did not see power, while heroes did. The martyr was the aborted hero. Martyrdom was also the Christian's and the woman's greatest crown. Jane adored the heroic, but having been trained in Christianity and the female duties of self-sacrifice and having known personal suffering from childhood, she felt martyrdom's appeal.[45]

Thus I intensify this inquiry by submitting that the majority of human services workers are women and that this kind of martyrdom that practitioners may be vulnerable to taking on is rooted in patriarchal religions and other cultural practices that have historically informed the larger culture. These forces are indeed challenging to unpack, but I know for me personally it can be very helpful to at least notice when I am voicing, internally and externally, a martyrdom narrative; I find it to be a narrative that does not often serve me or those around me very well.

Many change agents are ambivalent about self-care because it has arguably become another commodity of neoliberal capitalism, perpetuating an industry of narcissism, which simultaneously creates greater social disparity and perhaps distracts people from changing the system itself. The challenge here is to work with these concerns, acknowledge the paradoxes, and endeavor to move forward with the important work to be done. Thus these kinds of deep examinations are required if one is to advance and act on one's own (and others') best interests. Accordingly, this book challenges social practitioners and practitioners-in-training to examine the reasons why they may find themselves ambivalent about self-care, whether they see it as a form of selfishness or a waste of time, or something they may be prone to get obsessive about by working to achieve the perfect body or some form of spiritual transcendence. Within this complex terrain, the book offers a pathway—of inquiry, reflection, practice, and skill building—that can empower workers, clients, organizations, communities, and the wider world.

Healing Justice as Practice

Many helping professionals and social change agents find themselves working in contexts that fully embody the values of neoliberal global capitalism—commodification of people and natural resources, social welfare retrenchment, disembodiment, fixation on efficiency, overreliance on technology for problem-solving, and disconnection from each other and the nonhuman environment.[46] As such, many are struggling to deal with the disenfranchisement they (and the people they are working with or on behalf of) are feeling from institutions and services that are meant to lift people up. I have found that many of my social work students and social practitioners that I train are struggling with a painful dissonance between their ideals of social justice and human dignity on the one hand and the disappointing realities of contemporary social services provision on the other. Thus healing justice practices in the midst of this dissonance are desperately needed.

While many organizations and universities are beginning to recognize the need for self-care, their approaches tend to emphasize "managing" stress, are narrowly concerned with the individual, and limit their focus to the cognitive dimension of the self.[47] The approach to healing justice I offer here, however, is to *cultivate a relationship* with stress, *study its origins, acknowledge* the whole self, learn about our *personal and collective conditioning* that contributes to our dis-ease, and *engage in practices* that can *heal* and *transform* stress and internalized oppression for the highest good of ourselves, society, and the world in which we live. Taking this approach asks practitioners to investigate the cultural values and norms, economic systems, and organizational environments that they may have unconsciously adopted or that may be actively contributing to lack of well-being, addiction, anxiety, low self-esteem, and disconnection from others.

Some approaches to self-care are inclined to compartmentalize it into something that one only does with and on behalf of "the professional self."[48] On the contrary, healing justice attends to the whole person, including the nonprofessional self, as indeed there is a plethora of conscious and unconscious material from our personal lives and the wider culture that is driving our attitudes and behaviors in practice; it is all of this material that we are called to care for, heal, and transform. Healing justice may not necessarily change the world, but, if practiced well, it can, at the very least, strengthen one's capacities for transformative social practice.

A Journey Toward Wholeness

The human journey can be a journey of connection, transformation, and movement toward wholeness and wellness. Through mindfulness and compassion toward others, and oneself, it is possible to begin to sew together what is severed—the mind and the body, self and other, person and planet, and the material and the spiritual. We can go beyond just surviving and cultivate what positive psychology teaches, namely, the ability of humans to thrive and to find joy, meaning, and fulfillment in life[49] or what Aristotle referred to as "the good life."

The primary practice orientation of this book is focused on mindfulness. To be mindful is "to wake up, to recognize what is happening in the present moment."[50] Jon Kabat-Zinn has offered a very helpful definition of mindfulness: "Paying attention in a particular way: on purpose, in the present moment, and non-judgmentally."[51] When we are mindful, "our attention is not entangled in the past or future, and we are not judging or rejecting what is occurring at the moment. We are present. This kind of attention generates energy, clearheadedness, and joy."[52] To be sure, healing and transforming oppression, trauma, and burnout demands such energy and clearheadedness (along with action). Healing justice proposes that we bring our nonjudgmental awareness to what is asking for our kind attention *right here and now*.

The challenge for many practitioners is that when they take moments to slow down or inquire into how they are, or how a group they are working with is, they often do not like what they see. It is sometimes too painful to deal with and/or perhaps they do not have the proper support and conditions to attend to it. So they tend to deny, avoid, circumvent, or conquer that which they do not like about themselves and each other, uncomfortable feelings they do not want to feel, or conflict in their organizations or wider world. But, as the saying goes, "what we resist persists," and this book therefore invites the reader to make a conscious choice to develop a relationship with embodied experiences, thoughts, and feelings and try to befriend them as the path of healing justice and as a vital dimension of transformative social practice. In doing this, they can develop what has been called an integrative capability to use all of the information, sensations, and insights to learn from experience and respond in real time.[53] Instead of avoiding, the opportunity is to live life fully, "to live life as if each moment is important, as if each moment counted and could be worked with, even if it is a moment of pain, sadness, despair, or fear."[54] Rather than pushing one's truths away (and to be sure these truths are the intersubjective truths of our culture), perhaps it is the case that everything is grist for the mill and that actually all of one's "stuff"—personal and collective obsessions, fears, and problems—are phenomena to get curious about.

Philosopher and poet Mark Nepo offers a series of questions that can help illuminate the depth of inquiry required to engage in healing and transformative work. He asks,

> How do we respond to the tide of experience that sweeps into our ordinary lives? Do we respond to the unknown by being absent or being present? Do we hoard or give? Do we circumvent the truth or move through the truth? Do we withdraw and hide or stand in the open and seek connection? Do we view difficulty and suffering as isolating obstacles that exploit our weakness and stall our progress in life? Or do we view these incidents as transforming the waves of experience that are part of an ongoing emergence of who we are? Do we believe that life is a-pulling-apart we must survive or a constant rearrangement and putting together that we must surrender to? Do we run toward or from the bareness of being?[55]

Sometimes, and perhaps often, running toward the bareness of being is just too much. When this is true for you, you can cultivate compassion for yourself, for where you are in any given moment. When you are able though, you can take the opportunity to use the stressors of life—the confusion, the ambiguity, the intensity—to wake up to the moment. This kind of self-care is more than just trying to get through a difficult day in the trenches; the aspirations are much higher. By bringing awareness or mindfulness to that which we tend to reject, we are reminded of our humanity, our uniqueness, and, ironically, our strengths. It is ultimately something that can bring us closer to others. With proper support, and with great courage and humility, we can put all of our life experiences on the altar and allow them to guide us in the direction that we need to go. Rather than throwing it all away, we recycle and compost.

Putting It Into Practice
Inquiry

Reflect on your own personal experiences of coping with oppression, whether your own that may be a result of your gender identity, race/ethnicity, immigration status, ability, or sexual orientation, or that of others and the world around you. Where do you feel pain or lingering hurts around this? How does it impact your thinking? In what ways do your experiences coping with oppression impact the work you do? Jot down or share with someone anything that comes up with you and/or share with an individual or group.

Self-Care Practice Skill

In a seated or standing position, with your eyes open or closed, notice your own breathing. Do you notice it in your chest or belly or nostrils? What shape is the breath taking in your body? Or notice sensations in the body. Can you feel your hands touching the book, computer, or your lap? Can you feel the back of your legs touching your seat, or the feeling of your feet on the floor? You've just practiced mindfulness of the breath/body. Jot down or share with someone what you noticed and any challenges you had in noticing.

Experiment for a Day

This one is simple. Pick your favorite "go to" self-care practice, one that has been reliable for you over the years in terms of its ability to positively impact your body, mind, or spirit. It might be playing a game of tennis, cooking a healthy meal, or meeting up with a friend for a walk. Whatever it is, go do it—today, tomorrow, or sometime soon. Notice how you feel before, during, and after you do it. Share with someone—family, friend, or colleague—how it went for you.

2

Stress and the Self-Care Revolution

"Trauma is not just the result of major disasters. It does not happen to only some people. An undercurrent of trauma runs through ordinary life."

—MARK EPSTEIN, MD (2013)[1]

Case Study

Margarita has been an activist for as long as she can remember. Whether it was helping her brother, who has a disability, navigate and change unresponsive policies at their high school or working with at-risk youth at an afterschool program at her church, addressing injustice is in her bones. Moreover, she has always been the helper and mediator in her family, which has struggled to make ends meet and care for their child with a disability. After college, Margarita went to work at the Department of Social Services as a case worker for families struggling to overcome abuse and neglect. She carries a very large caseload in a system she deems oppressive and disempowering to poor people.

Six years later, Margarita has found that, throughout her workday, she has developed the habit of dealing with the stressors that come her way (e.g., a traumatized child, paperwork deadlines, and worries about her own family) by snacking on junk food excessively and then feeling bad about it afterwards. There always seems to be birthday cake or donuts around the office, and eating temporarily lifts her mood and gives her energy. Now, at age 29, she finds herself disconnected from and uncomfortable in her body, anxious and depressed, and feeling like she is in a rut. She has tried to change her habits but feels like the stress is just too overwhelming, and so she goes back to her old patterns. She desperately wants to do something different for herself as she sees these same patterns in her family members who used eating as a way to cope with the stress of immigration and the hostile and challenging environment that they found themselves living and working in.

A few months ago, a friend of hers from college mentioned that journaling has really helped her to process her experiences and find new solutions to what is going on in her life and work. Margarita remembered that she kept a journal in high school about her life, even writing some poems now and again. She had written the poems in her mother tongue of Spanish so that others in her high school wouldn't know what she was writing. As she thought about journaling, a light bulb turned on for her, and she decided to give it a try again.

That night after work, she bought herself a new journal and wrote about her day. She heard once that to create a new habit that you should do it for three weeks and then it will be ingrained in your system, so she committed herself to it and did it. At first, none of her behaviors changed, but she was learning about herself and her environment. She shared some of her insights with her friend, and they committed to supporting each other in the process. She realized that she had been experiencing anxiety and anger and it was so uncomfortable that eating seemed to be the only way to calm herself down. She also started writing poems again, some of which expressed a lot of anger toward a system she thought should be supporting its workers, and the families they serve, in more empowering ways.

Journaling has led to some positive results for Margarita, including finding alternative behaviors to deal with stress before, during, and after her work. For example, she has started a lunchtime walking group at her office and is beginning to feel better in her own body. She listens to uplifting music in the car between home visits. And she is bringing her own healthier snacks to work with her. She and her fellow walkers are also beginning to have conversations with coworkers and supervisors about ways that they can create a culture of self-care and reduce their workload.

Understanding Stress

A recent meme going around social media shows a picture of a doctor and the words: "Feeling sad and depressed? Are you anxious? Worried about the future? Feeling isolated and alone? You might be suffering from CAPITALISM." This tongue-in-cheek image brings attention to the impact that the global economy is having on poor, working, and middle-class people who are losing out on the promises that capitalism would lift everyone up. Prior to the 1960s there was virtually no research on the subject of stress. Today, however, it is a topic that is being studied and discussed extensively, both in the general population and in the helping fields in relation to practitioner burnout.[2] While there are some exceptions, medical and other scientific research tends to avoid making connections between stress and the global neoliberal milieu, instead isolating variables and ignoring the underlying causes of stress. At any rate, learning about what stress is and how it manifests can be useful for the purposes of healing justice, which is, at least in part, concerned with the alleviation of stress.

Stress can be understood as a state of anxiety that occurs when one's perceptions of situations and responsibilities exceed one's abilities to cope with them, as was the case with Margarita.[3] Scholars have identified four types of stress: physical stress, psychological stress, psychosocial stress, and psychospiritual stress.[4] This book is concerned with the alleviation all of these types of stress. The sources of stress for our primitive ancestors were things like becoming prey for a creature stronger and faster than them, starvation, childbirth, and dying from parasites in unclean drinking water. Most practitioners do not have to worry about these kinds of troubles. They still have serious challenges to deal with, though, including real traumas, discrimination, and health problems faced by their family members, clients, and themselves. Some scholars and therapists have noted that stress about the state of the world, particularly worries about the state of the economy and degradation of the environment, has a real and significant impact on people.[5,6] Many of the immediate stressors that people face today tend to be concerned with feeling overwhelmed by emotions in relation to responsibilities and relationships. In the big evolutionary picture, the kind of sustained psychological stress is a fairly new phenomenon.

The contemporary stress load is also exacerbated by what has been called *technostress*,[7] the inability to deal with the rapid pace of technology, or *digiphrenia*, the tension between the artificial reality of digital bombardment and the real flesh and blood earthly existence of *now*. According to Douglas Rushkoff,[8] who coined the phrase, digiphrenia happens because

> we are *always*-on. Our boss isn't the guy in the corner office, but a PDA in our pocket. Our taskmaster is depersonalized and internalized – and even more rigorous than the union busters of yesterday. There is no safe time. If we are truly to take time away from the program, we feel we must disconnect altogether and live "off the grid," as if we were members of a different, predigital era.

People experience this kind of stress when they cannot cope with technology in a healthy manner or find coherence between the frantic pace of the digital environment and a salutary, naturally rhythmic way of living in the world.

Due to the rapid rate at which information flows, many practitioners feel compelled to work faster. Higher caseloads in social services organizations, digitized client tracking systems, having to do more with less, and high needs in the community exacerbate this. Practitioners may experience information overload, engage in habitual multitasking, and become addicted to technology. To be sure, technological addiction is not exactly their fault. Wired devices are programmed by tech companies with algorithms that are designed to get people addicted to them, as advertising is uniquely curated for each person, resulting in more clicks, more purchasing, and more profits for a few.[9] The digital interface preys on the natural human tendency toward seeking out what is new, compelling, and shiny. The phenomenon has been referred to as "the race to the bottom of the brain stem."[10] Moreover, digital engagement is largely a disembodied experience, and thus it has a tendency to further alienate people from their bodies, emotions, and spirits. Indeed, manifestations of this kind of stress can be physical (e.g., headaches or neck pain), emotional (e.g., anxiety or irritability), and existential.[11]

Stress-filled living has become the norm in the dominant culture. Some medical professionals have gone so far as to describe modern day stress as an epidemic.[12] The American Psychological Association[13] recently reported on a study that revealed that the top five stressors for Americans, in order, are money, work, the economy, family responsibilities, and personal health concerns. The 2013 Everest College Study on Work Stress found that 8 out of 10 employed Americans reported they were stressed out on the job, citing heavier workloads and low pay as the top sources of work stress.[14] Of note, this study revealed that women are more likely than men to say that low wages are the most stressful aspect of their work. The stress for people who are unemployed (about 9 million people in the United States at the time of the study) is also significant, as the research shows that there are unique physical and mental health risks for those who are unemployed.

Some research has revealed that people are even more stressed at home than work (especially women) with so many duties to attend to, including childcare, eldercare, cooking, and housework.[15] Furthermore, a body of research has revealed that racism and racial stress are related to negative health and mental health outcomes in populations who are the target of such oppression including Black, Latinx, and Indigenous people.[16] One of the important lessons from this research, in relation to the healing justice framework, is that stress is not something to pathologize at an individual level. Instead, one's understanding needs to broaden, as stress is clearly a social phenomenon, intertwined with social values and a system that legitimizes dehumanized environments of efficiency, overwork, and marginalization of vulnerable groups.

In her book on the history of exhaustion, Anna Schaffner reveals that humans have actually been thinking about and theorizing exhaustion for centuries, even though stress-filled living seems so unique to us.[17] Authors of the past tended to attribute exhaustion to advances in technology—increased consumption of luxury goods in the eighteenth century and the faster pace that trains, electricity, and the telegraph brought in the late nineteenth century. To be sure, this collective concern with exhaustion is rooted not only in a sense of being overwhelmed by technology but by a timeless anxiety about aging, the loss of effectiveness in the world, and death.

The Impact of Stress

The American Institute of Stress estimates that 75% to 90% of all primary care physician visits are related to stress.[18] Indeed, stress and maladaptive health and lifestyle behaviors are clearly connected. According to former US Surgeon General Julius Richmond,

> Of the ten leading causes of illness and death in the U.S., seven could be greatly reduced if the following lifestyle habits were modified—alcohol abuse, lack of exercise, poor diet, smoking, and unhealthy maladaptive responses to stress and tension.[19]

Long-term, or chronic stress, is also the breeding ground for disease, as cortisol levels rise, blood sugar levels increase, and the immune system becomes suppressed.[20] At a low-grade level, stress can result in sleep problems, lack of mental clarity and focus, weight gain or loss, headaches, anxiety, and digestive problems.[21] Eventually, this kind of chronic stress increases risk of major diseases, such as ulcers, heart disease, cancer, and hypertension.[22]

There is extensive data on the prevalence of stress and burnout among social workers and other helping professionals. For example, a study of 751 social workers found that about three-fourths reported having trouble with burnout during their careers.[23] Other studies have shown 60% of gerontological social workers and 62% of child protective workers experienced emotional exhaustion.[24] This kind of stress is associated with negative health and mental health outcomes, including depression, decreased immune functioning, and poor health behaviors.[25] "Poor health behavior"—perhaps not exactly a term that helps to explain the social and systemic factors that contribute to poor health—was certainly the kind of challenge that Margarita was facing.

Clearly, social change agents and other helping professionals experience all of these kinds of stressors of contemporary living. And yet their stress is exacerbated by their unique contexts, which demand selflessness, exposure to trauma, and the ongoing dissonance between social injustice and the realities of how social services and social change organizations actually operate, such as what Margarita identified. In its extreme form, this kind of stress is often referred to as burnout. *Burnout* is a "prolonged psychological response to chronic workplace stressors and is theorized to include three dimensions: emotional exhaustion, depersonalization or cynicism, and diminished personal accomplishment."[26] Scholars have sought to distinguish between burnout and compassion fatigue, noting that compassion fatigue is the result of working with trauma and suffering but that burnout points to the larger social and organizational context as the culprit.[27] Later in this book, in the chapter on healing justice organizations, I discuss the structural and organizational causes of burnout (and offer remedies for it) more extensively.

It is no wonder that people are willing to try so many things to help them reduce their stress load. Certainly, stress reduction has become a very popular and lucrative industry. For example, massage therapy brings in $13 billion per year.[28] The 2016 Yoga in America study found that the number of yoga practitioners had increased to over 36 million, up from 20 million in 2012, while spending on yoga rose from $10 billion to $16 billion in that same time period.[29] A significant amount of that money is spent on high-dollar yoga clothing and accessories.

Thus the global economic system that exacerbates stress with low wages, overly competitive environments, and digiphrenia also creates opportunities to aggressively market remedies to alleviate such stress, whether it is diet pills or fancy yoga pants. To be sure, the "self-care revolution" is a big money-maker, and not for the frontline people who are doing the work—yoga teachers, Lululemon retail store employees, or pedicurists—but the owners and stockholders of the companies who are creating their empires.

Stress and Your Relationship with Time

Many practitioners experience, or experience regularly, what has come to be called a "time famine." This is the state when one feels constantly rushed, with looming deadlines, and the sense that there is not enough time in the day to do the things that one needs to do. Many people often find themselves in a hurry and the mantra becomes "hurry up." To deal with this anxiety and to "manage our time," according to Arianna Huffington[30] in her book *Thrive: The Third Metric to Redefining Success and Creating a Life of Wellbeing, Wisdom and Wonder,*

> We rigidly schedule ourselves, rushing from meeting to meeting, event to event, constantly trying to save a bit of time here, a bit there. We download apps for productivity and eagerly click on articles with time-saving life hacks. We try to shave a few seconds off our daily routine, in hopes that we can create enough space to schedule yet another meeting or appointment that will help us climb the ladder of success.

For many people, this situation leads to emotional and physical depletion, dissatisfaction with life and work, and chronic anxiety.

We live by the clock. We notice the clock easily a hundred times a day, whether it is checking our phone, seeing the clock on our computer, or looking at it on the dashboard of the car, not to mention watches and wall clocks.[31] Researchers have studied this way of "living by the clock." One study focused on participants in a vigorous yoga class, dividing them into two groups—one group with a clock in the room and the other without.[32] The group with a clock in the room did not perform the postures as well, as they kept looking at the clock and gave up on the postures more easily. They also left the class feeling less inspired than the group without a clock. Other research has shown that people who are overly concerned with clock time tend to find less pleasure in life, are less creative, and are not as well connected to their emotions.[33] For therapists or other practitioners billing for services, the 50-minute hour of therapy, which is clearly an arbitrary time frame, forces the therapist and client to shoe horn experience within rigid parameters. It would seem then that this aspect of the dominant culture is having a negative impact on practitioners, which in turn challenges their ability to be tuned into their own and others' whole selves and to be able to respond creatively.

Another indicator of the lack of synchronization with time is the tendency to engage in activities that are out of alignment with the rhythms of nature, or circadian rhythms. Circadian rhythms are physical, mental, and behavioral patterns that roughly follow a 24-hour cycle, related primarily to light and darkness in the environment.[34] Most humans on the planet today have false light available to them, allowing them to work or play late into the night, a time when their bodies and minds actually need restoration and rejuvenation through sleep.[35] People may be eating and drinking at midnight, a time when the digestive system might be better off resting. In addition, the globalized food system allows people to eat food out of season, like tomatoes in the middle of winter. And, because the neoliberal capitalist culture is concerned with quickness and efficiency, such as fast food, instantly downloadable music, and never-ending news, people lose touch with a felt sense of the analog world, how long it actually takes to do things, and a sense of linear time.

Healing Your Relationship with Time

How can practitioners work within such a context and strive to resist the social forces of hurry, busyness, and stress? To begin to answer this question, I offer a few antidotes to this fractured relationship with time and indeed to stress in general: (a) mindfulness, (b) savoring pleasurable moments, and (c) conscious use of time. While doing these things will not change the social conditions that contribute to this kind of time-related stress, practitioners may ultimately find that engaging in these kinds of healing justice practices, some of which I share in forthcoming chapters, cultivates a greater sense of empowerment in their lives and work. Next I describe briefly these three preliminary practices.

Mindfulness is a central topic in this book and one that I will continue to focus on in detail throughout. Drawing on the basic definition of mindfulness (i.e., remembering to notice what is happening in any given moment[36]) can help one "heal their relationship with time," as yoga teacher Matthew Remski has said.[37] There is something about honing into the smallest, minutest details of a moment that creates a sense of connection and groundedness, as well as expansiveness. When you notice the thrumming of the computer at your desk, or the temperature of your own skin, you may find a greater sense of relaxation, creating a sense that things are slowing down. On the other hand, you may find such noticings exacerbate your stress level, so it may be helpful to find some detail to notice that has a more positive affect on you.

Savoring pleasurable moments means that one allows oneself to really *have* the brief moments throughout the day when one experiences pleasure. Perhaps it is tasting something delicious, or the laughter one shares with a client or colleague, or the feeling of crawling into a comfortable bed after a long day. Rather than anticipating the next thing that is coming, one can pause and lean into such experiences a bit more fully. When one marinates in the feelings and sensations, one can lock in and rack up positive experiences to counteract the tendency toward thinking about the past or future, or perhaps an unconscious belief that "I do not deserve pleasure." The positive psychology movement has been influential in helping to shed light on positive emotions and happiness. Rick Hanson, PhD, calls this "taking in the good," or "hardwiring happiness," an evidence-based practice, grounded in mindfulness traditions, that he has developed to cultivate happiness.[38] Doing this regularly can actually change the neural structure of the brain. Readers will have the opportunity to learn more about the neuroscience research behind and techniques for engaging in this practice, as it is developed more fully in forthcoming chapters.

A recent study found that giving time to others actually increased one's subjective sense of having a lot of time.[39] Human services workers and social change agents, of course, give a significant amount of their time to others. Clearly, the time one spends supporting a client in distress, mentoring a new community organizer, or volunteering to be on a new committee can give one a feeling of satisfaction. When one is more satisfied, one is less likely to be so obsessed with time. But, are we always truly present for the people to whom we are giving our time? Moreover, is filling our time up with more and more activities supportive of our healing? In my experience, I have noticed that when I am not giving my full attention to someone, it is either because of an underlying belief that I am too busy and that I have other more important things to do or it is because I am preoccupied with some kind of stressor. These may be signals that it might be time to step away, take a break, or find some down time. Of course doing this is a privilege and one that not all practitioners (nor indeed the people they work with) universally possess. But the ability to cultivate more consciousness about how one spends one's time, as well as the capability to set boundaries for self-care, can be critical, and indeed transformative, skills for practitioners to nurture.

When I can offer my attention to a person as fully as I am able, not only does that person benefit by being seen and heard more fully, but I benefit too as I become more connected and less self-involved (and less worried about what time it is). Likewise, when I am able to ask for a timeout, everyone can reap the rewards, or at least not be harmed any further by my agitation. Perhaps a time study of your day could be helpful, noting how you spend each day (including time spent online) and thus allowing you to gain more consciousness about what you are doing with your life. In the chapter on the healing justice organization, I discuss in more detail the need to create changes in organizational structures and cultures so that these kinds of personal changes can be more possible and fruitful. Overall, our fractured relationship with time is a symptom not only of the era we live in—the culture and economic system—but of the human tendency toward distraction from being present in the moment, an evolutionary development of the brain. By engaging in a path that centers mindful self-care, it is possible for practitioners to begin to find more satisfaction, which positively impacts their ability to sustain their social change work.

Chronic Stress and Stress Reduction

The autonomic nervous system of the human body has an intricate structure in place to help people deal with stress, known as the sympathetic nervous system.[40] This system is connected to the "fight, flight, or freeze" response. It kicks in to make people more alert and aware when they are in the middle of a scary situation, like when someone steps out to cross the street and a car nearly hits him or her, as the driver slams on the brakes just in the nick of time. Adrenaline hormones start pumping, the breath shortens, and the heart rate rises. It is a completely normal response that all humans experience. Once the situation is over, the body begins to return to stability, also known as homeostasis or allostasis, as the parasympathetic nervous system, the natural mechanism that the body has for self-soothing, takes over, allowing us to be relaxed again.[41] When this parasympathetic nervous system is active, the digestive system is functioning, breathing slows down, cell repair can take place, and the immune system can function. In the book *Why Zebras Don't Get Ulcers*, Robert Sapolsky juxtaposes the human experience of worry and stress to that of the acute physical stress experienced by animals.[42] Consider that when an animal is being chased in the wild and makes it out of the situation alive, it shakes itself off (literally) and then returns to its normal business. Unlike humans, the zebra does not start obsessing over what happened, go and tell all its friends about what a jerk the predator was, or take it personally in any way. This kind of human behavior can lead to a form of toxicity known as *chronic stress*.[43]

Because of humans' natural inclination to avoid stressors, they are prone to go to great lengths to keep an eye out for trouble, making them more tuned into and interested in negative situations and experiences (e.g., car wrecks, gossip, criticism, etc.). This phenomenon has been referred to as a built-in *negativity bias*.[44] To make the assumption that things out there are threatening was helpful to our ancestors as they worked hard to avoid predators and starvation. But when there is no actual threat, this inclination toward negativity becomes a cognitive distortion of reality. Thus people habitually try to avoid the pain of more stress by approaching compulsive pleasures to alleviate discomfort, which is exactly the pattern that Margarita found herself in.

There is an important emotional element at play when considering chronic stress too, as people have a tendency to get caught up in, if not addicted to, their survival emotions associated with the instinctual/reptilian part of the brain (e.g., fear, greed, jealousy, anger, and desire).[45] Practitioners may find themselves repeating the story about what an annoying coworker did to them to anyone who will listen, and yet it does not often relieve them of any stress; it tends to reinforce negative and aversive feelings. Of course, feeling emotions is normal and good, part of the pathos of humanity. However, rehashing, being overwhelmed by, and obsessing over emotions and storylines disempowers. Indeed, sometimes people are imagining problems for themselves that do not actually exist. As Mark Twain said, "I have suffered a great many misfortunes, most of which never happened."

These phenomena reveal the ways that the mind and body work together, as chronic stress can result in an overactive sympathetic nervous symptom response that can result in mental health problems, reduced immune system functioning, and increased inflammation. It is also important to distinguish here between stress, chronic stress, and trauma. Trauma, posttraumatic stress disorder, and complex trauma (relational trauma that is cumulative) are unresolved responses to a life-threatening situation.[46] As noted earlier, trauma can result in avoidance, hypervigilance, and intrusive thoughts.

Risk, Resilience, and Coping

Stress and stress reduction can be more fully understood by bringing in some of the research on resilience and coping. A note of caution about the risk and resilience literature is in order though. Namely, this literature

often fails (though not always) to contextualize risk within the larger systemic forces that cause and perpetuate it. This happens at the same time
that it advocates for individualized coping remedies and resilience building, thus failing to consider and attend to the power that community organizing and systems change could play in eliminating the risk in the first
place. Nevertheless, there can be something to learn from this research
that can be helpful for those who want to consciously bring more awareness to their difficult and painful experiences, as well as to understand
how to lessen the burden they have on them.

Childhood experiences of trauma, and even prenatal stress, factor
into one's risk for health, mental health, and other problems. The ACES
research has identified 10 adverse childhood experiences that may lead to
problems related to child development, risky behaviors, substance abuse,
disease, and even early death. These experiences are physical abuse, sexual abuse, emotional abuse, physical neglect, emotional neglect, mother
treated violently, substance misuse within the household, household mental illness, parental separation or divorce, and incarcerated household
member.[47] To contextualize these findings, it may be helpful here to invoke
French social theorist Michel Foucault's concept of biopower. He writes,

> If the development of the great instruments of the state, as *institu-*
> *tions* of power, ensured the maintenance of production relations, the
> rudiments of anatomo- and bio-politics, created in the eighteenth
> century as *techniques* of power present at every level of the social
> body and utilised by very diverse institutions (the family and the
> army, schools and the police, individual medicine and the adminis-
> tration of collective bodies), operated in the sphere of economic pro-
> cesses, their development, and the forces working to sustain them.[48]

Notice he mentions the family, which embodies the patriarchal and capitalist milieu in which these ACES transpire, thus paving the way, for example, for abuse of those who have less power in the family or, for families
that are poor, for neglect. Thus an understanding of the unique challenges
and tendencies that a person may have, as well as resources and strengths
he or she possesses, is always embedded in a particular social location
within this dominant social order.

In terms of resilience to such risks, research has shown that individual characteristics and behaviors, such as optimism, active coping
skills, humor, physical exercise, prosocial behavior such as altruism, and

mindfulness are all associated with higher levels of resilient functioning.[49] Studies have shown that genetic factors also play a role in why some people are better able to handle such adversity, trauma, and stress than others.[50] Connection to a community, culture, and strong social networks appear to be key to resilient coping as well. Chapter 8 focuses in more detail on the role of community in facilitating the healing of social practitioners.

To cope with the stress in our lives we learn how to self-soothe so that we can calm down and regulate our emotions. We begin this practice in infancy, perhaps by sucking on our fingers, toes, or pacifier, and later finding solace in a favorite blanket or stuffed animal. As we become adults we develop different habits of self-soothing and emotion regulation, some of it geared internally, such as breathing deeply or changing the way we think about a situation, and some of it geared externally, like having a cup of warm tea or talking to a friend. Emotion regulation can entail a range of behaviors, including changing the situation or stimuli that is bothering us. We may bring our attention toward the emotion, such as through rumination or worry, or away from the emotion, by distracting ourselves with other activities. We may also reappraise the meaning of a situation through the use of humor or modulate our responses by changing the effects of the event or emotion on our system, such as through exercise.

Even if you do not think you are very good at handling stress, you are actually really quite skilled at it. *Indeed, humans are naturally inclined to self-care.* When people feel the stress of being cold, they reach for a sweater or jacket or turn up the heat. When they feel the stress of hunger, they eat. When people are lonely or need resources, they reach out to people around them and draw strength and support from family, friends, and community. These strengths-oriented perspectives are especially important as one considers those who are marginalized or oppressed in society, who are often viewed as helpless, isolated, or dependent on the system. Carol Stack's seminal anthropological study of the survival skills of low-income African Americans identified the ways in which they utilized extended kinship networks to take care of each other by exchanging childcare, food, diapers, and other resources.[51] Care in the context of community is what human beings have always done, as their naturally tendency is arguably toward cooperation and care, rather than toward individualism and competitiveness.

Recently, a social worker who was a participant in a workshop I was giving on self-care said that she has a long drive to work and spends the whole time singing at the top of her lungs. She explained that this was why she was always in a good mood when she gets to work. Until the workshop, she had never before thought of what she was doing as a form of self-care. But we really are predisposed to take care of ourselves. Even when one considers some of their more unwholesome coping skills, like those that Margarita found herself engaged in, these behaviors are still coming from the pure intention of protecting oneself from stress.

Without a doubt, one can learn to work more consciously and effectively with stress. This is empowering and is arguably a form of resistance to a culture that circulates messages that everyone must be busy, harried, and stressed out all the time to be fully human (and thus buy all of the products that could make it all better—a latte, a faster computer, or an expensive vacation). Consciously working with stress, which is a fundamental way to practice healing justice, represents an opportunity to walk the talk of transformative social change and treat yourself with the kind of dignity and respect that you would wish for everyone.

Stress Reduction Practices

There is a growing body of research on social workers, therapists, medical personnel, and other helping professionals that establishes a clear link between certain behaviors and stress reduction. Some of these activities include time in nature, time with friends, creative arts, vigorous exercise, mindfulness, conscious breathing, and journaling.[52-54] Studies have demonstrated, for instance, that journaling can actually improve physical health, relieve stress, reduce high blood pressure, and improve sleep. Writing about stressful events can reduce the negative impact of the stressor by helping the writer to gain greater perspective and become more empowered, as was the case with Margarita. It is important to keep in mind that such studies, like many about mindfulness and yoga that I review later in the book, are limited, particularly in terms of their small sample sizes and their failure to use randomized control trials (considered the gold standard in scientific research).

Perhaps more important than the evidence-based research on self-care is what your own personal experience (and the wisdom of those around you) can teach you. For me, I know that walking with my dog or drinking a cup of warm tea are stress reducers. During my workday, sometimes I find myself in my car in a parking lot between meetings. I try to use such moments to restore myself, by closing my eyes and engaging in two or three minutes of meditation, feeling into my body and leaning into my breath. All such palliative practices can take the sharp edges off the effects of feeling beleaguered by an abundance of commitments or overwhelming emotions or just feeling fatigued.

The types of stress reduction practices one uses will vary according to what one is experiencing in the moment. When one is feeling anxious or overwhelmed by one's worries, restless energy, and ambition, it may be necessary to *downregulate* (i.e., to gently cajole energy to move downward toward the earth), creating more of a sense of heaviness or groundedness in the system. An example of downregulating would be emphasizing the exhale when you breathe (even sighing) or bringing your awareness into your feet if you are standing, or to your backside if you are sitting. If one is feeling underwhelmed, depressed, or lethargic, it may be time to *upregulate* (i.e., to invite one's energy upwards, toward the sky), creating more of a sense of lightness or flowing energy in the system. Examples include taking deep inhales by filling up the chest with breath and even holding it in there for a few seconds before letting it go, lifting and/or stretching arms up overhead, going for a vigorous walk, or laughing.

Self-care practice invites practitioners to become skillful in ways to self-soothe in the moment, while *healing justice* is a practice that summons one to pause longer and stay with what is happening in order to learn about the nature and origins of one's thoughts, emotions, and behavior patterns in relation to internal and environmental causes and conditions. Healing justice also means that, when appropriate, practitioners teach others, especially those who have less access to wellness, these kinds of exercises and inquiries. This is discussed in more detail in Chapter 11. In addition, vital to healing justice is that people learn what their limits are (i.e., realize when they do not have the capacity to be with particular emotions, people, or circumstances and thus need to self-soothe, check out a little bit, or set a boundary).

Setting boundaries can be a lifeline for many people who may have been conditioned to please others, to overextend themselves, or to lose touch with an empowered voice. I have encouraged my students to set personal boundaries for themselves when it is appropriate and possible. For example, if they are triggered or too troubled by certain populations or settings (e.g., people who are severely mentally ill, children, or a prison environment), I support them in gaining clarity about the kinds of work they might not be willing to do when they are getting matched for an internship and to communicate this. In my opinion, it does not serve them well to over-ride their needs and intuition at the beginning of their careers. Overall, it is important that people stay realistic about where they are and any tenden-cies they may have toward pushing themselves too hard or meeting socially constructed expectations. As meditation teacher Ajahn Chah said, "Don't pretend you have the capacity of a 10-ton truck when you really only have the capacity of a wheelbarrow."

When I feel overwhelmed by sadness or depression, just to become aware of it and not judge myself for it is a big deal. Sometimes I have the capacity to stay with it and ride the wave; other times I may put on some upbeat music like reggae to lift my mood. Still, there are times when it feels like too much, or I have trouble noticing it at all and/or accepting it. In these cases, I may find myself engaging in less wholesome behaviors, such as watching a legion of reality TV episodes. None of these responses are "good" or "right" or "bad" or "wrong." It is just where I am in the moment. The invitation is to remember to try and stay aware of what is happening, what one's intentions are, what one's responses are, and to continue to inquire into the matter with curiosity and compassion. Healing justice practice means that one learns about the causes and conditions that may create such difficult feelings and the role that the larger environment plays in our personal realities. As people become more connected to them-selves and their intuition, they can come to know what might be whole-some action for them in a given moment or situation, which in some cases may involve doing nothing. It is my experience that if I stay committed to being mindful without judgment, I stand a much better chance of gravitat-ing toward that which is wholesome.

Healing Justice as Revolutionary Act

To begin to unhook from habitual unconscious patterns that can aggra-vate chronic stress, practitioners can cultivate mindfulness through self-awareness of feelings, thoughts, situations, and responses. Specific skills for developing various types of mindfulness are offered in the second part of this book. Ultimately, whole self-presence can create more open-ness, rather than the smallness and tightness of suffering and reactivity. With more space, one can gain insight into oneself and the environment and can begin to make choices that make one feel more whole and better equipped to do the work of helping others and creating social change.

Obviously, stress reduction and mindfulness alone are not going to transform the world; it is necessary to speak out, act, organize, and take risks to try and make that happen. But healing justice is a path of inquiry that invites curiosity about yourself and the histories and realities of the social systems around you (family, community, schools, the economy, etc.). All of these elements have a role in creating who you are and what is transpiring in any given moment. As well, healing justice is a path that asks practitioners to practice nonjudgment and compassion for their own aversive, and perhaps obsessive, thought and behavioral patterns and the suffering these patterns can cause them as well as the people around them. As one engages in or continues on a healing journey, not only does compassion for oneself beget more compassion, but it can slowly grow into more empathy for others, as the research evidence on the associations between self-compassion and empathy are revealing.[55,56]

One could say that this kind of self-care is countercultural, and indeed, a revolutionary act. Learning to take better care of and heal each other and ourselves with benevolence could pave the way for the transformation of our communities and planet. Perhaps as much as anything, this is what social change agents and human services professionals are called to do at this moment in time. Many people are living lives such that the idea of self-care does not even exist; proactively implementing some of the self-care practices offered in this book into one's life would be completely impossible. For those of us who have some resources and time in our lives, besides taking care of our families and ourselves, healing justice implies that we help others to take care of themselves. As such, social change agents and helping professionals have the ethical duty to advocate for, organize with, and serve others such that stress reduction and self-care practices are available to the most vulnerable. Only when everyone has these practices available will social transformation be possible. Furthermore, if you find yourself drawn to sharing the discourses and practices of holistic self-care, I encourage you to do it consciously, in a way that is culturally sensitive and empowering. The food, music, movement practices, spiritual activities, and community building that are healing to me will not necessarily resonate with you, a colleague, or client. In the end, though, the charge is to cultivate a world where everyone can sit down and enjoy nourishing food; has time in their day to meditate, worship, dance, or sing; and can experience the full range of human emotions in a manner that fully expresses who they are.

Putting It Into Practice
Inquiry

Close your eyes and reflect on a time when you took care of yourself. This may be a time when you were sick with a cold or the flu and made the decision to stay home from work and allow yourself rest and fluids. Or recall the feeling of taking a warm bath. Next, think of a time when you felt taken care of. Perhaps it is as simple as a coworker bringing you a hot cup of coffee on a cold day or a loved one who made you dinner after a long day. Finally, think about a time when you were taking care of someone else—making your children breakfast or supporting a person with a disability while they testified about funding cuts. See if you can feel into these experiences and notice if there are any commonalities or differences about these three different types of experiences. There are no right or wrong answers. Notice too how you feel about each of these experiences and if you have any beliefs or inclinations about them, such as attachment or aversion. Consider your own social location as you inquire into this and the role that culture, social systems, and the economy have on your experiences. Journal about or share with another person anything that comes up for you with this exercise.

Self-Care Practice Skill

You will need a towel and a small amount of oil (sesame, grapeseed, olive, or coconut are good ones) or body lotion for this exercise. This is a self-massage practice called *abhyanga*, literally meaning "oil massage" in Sanskrit, and it originates from Ayurvedic medicine (the indigenous medicine of India). Seated on the floor or in a chair, take off your shoes and socks and set a small towel on the floor. Put about a teaspoon or so of oil in your hand and begin to massage the oil into one of your feet. Cover the entire foot, gently pressing your fingers and thumb into the sole of the foot to release tension. Notice how it feels. Take big, deep, "letting go" breaths as you do this. See if you can cultivate a sense of appreciation for your foot, as you cover the whole area of the foot repeatedly, acknowledging all the support and steps it has given you (and helped those you serve). Put that foot on the floor/towel and begin doing the same massage technique with the other foot. When you are finished, close your eyes and allow the experience to integrate, inviting awareness and inquiry into how your feet and whole body feels.

Experiment for a Day

For one day, keep a care journal. You will pay attention to the ways in which (a) you take care of yourself, (b) others take care of you, and (c) you take care of others. Create three columns on a piece of paper with each of these categories as a header. During the day, or at the end of the day looking back, jot down moments of care. For example, brushing your teeth can go into category (a), your colleague buying you lunch goes into category (b), and doing your family's laundry could go in category (c). You get to define what counts as "care." Reflect on or share with someone what you learned from this experiment.

3

The Whole Self

"A human being is a part of the whole, called by us 'Universe,' a part limited in time and space. He experiences himself, his thoughts and feelings as something separated from the rest, a kind of optical delusion of his consciousness. This delusion is a kind of prison for us, restricting us to our personal desires and to affection for a few persons nearest to us. Our task must be to free ourselves from this prison by widening our circle of compassion to embrace all living creatures and the whole of nature in its beauty. Nobody is able to achieve this completely, but the striving for such achievement is in itself a part of the liberation and a foundation for inner security."

—ALBERT EINSTEIN (1879–1955)

Case Study

Stephan was a busy and compassionate environmental and racial justice activist who worked as a community gardening educator with urban youth. He was also a full-time social work student, requiring him to do an internship that he was completing at a local high school. He was the father of a four-year old girl, Kahley, whom he spent time with on the weekends. He was passionate about everything happening in his life, but he didn't feel like he was doing anything particularly well. His regular state was a sense of being both wired and tired at the same time; he often felt overwhelmed; and he succumbed to colds and sinus infections regularly. He pushed himself with caffeine and junk food during the day and tried to de-compress from the stress with alcohol in the evenings. He averaged four to five hours of sleep per night.

One day, toward the end of the semester, it all came crashing in. Stephan literally could not get out of bed; he was exhausted and his body ached. After some rest, a friend suggested a naturopathic doctor who diagnosed him with adrenal fatigue. The doctor recommended changing his diet, sleeping at least eight hours a day, and stress reduction. Part of him wanted to implement the changes, but part of him liked something about his old way; it was familiar and it matched his view that he was put in this world to be an agent of change, not part of the self-involved bourgeoisie. He didn't have the time (or the money) to make himself "bro" protein smoothies, go to the gym, or sleep eight hours; his community was in crisis.

One early summer evening, with this ambivalent attitude toward his recovery racking his mind, he found himself at the community garden where he worked. He had taken a temporary leave of absence, but it was after-hours and he wanted to check in on how the gardens were looking. He saw that the gardens were in excellent shape. Everything was watered, weeded, and looking happy and healthy. He felt ambivalent about this too, pleased that everything was okay but a little hurt that everything functioned so well without him.

He sat down on the ground next to one of the beds and put his hands in the earth, running them through the soil as it fell through his fingers. He started to weep. He couldn't believe how good the cool dirt felt on his hands. He felt like he belonged to the earth and the earth belonged to him. He sensed a calm that he hadn't experienced since he was a child working in his grandfather's vegetable garden. He understood that the answer he was looking for was right in front of him.

Stephan's love of nature and the earth was what initially inspired him to get involved in environmental justice work, and so he made some important decisions for himself. For the time being, while finishing his degree, he moved in with a friend to save money. He stepped down as environmental educator and took the position of part-time gardener. He began reading books about mindful gardening and practiced it regularly, teaching the practice to his colleagues and friends, too. Gradually, he started to spend less time drinking, a little more time sleeping, more time cooking the food he brought home from the garden, and more time with Kahley.

He went back to the naturopath who recommended a holistic counselor in his office. He asked if they would accept payment on a sliding scale based on his income, and they agreed. The counselor invited him into an inquiry about several important issues, including a somatic exploration around the joy he felt from his connection to the outdoors, his beliefs around being so busy and being needed by others, and the relationship between his own health and healing and that of the world. While Stephan still struggles with taking care of himself, these have become lifelong inquiries for him.

Introduction

What or who is it exactly that practitioners are called to heal and care for if they are to embrace healing justice as a path forward? Is it their bodies? their minds? their communities? the environment? their spirits? In this chapter, I define, discuss, and explore what I mean by the whole self. The conclusions form the basis of the approach to holistic self-care and healing justice that the book encompasses. To begin this exploration, I analyze the dominant culture's tendency (including the culture of public and nonprofit organizations) to over-rely on cognition and to downplay or ignore the body, emotions, and spirit. Stephan, like many of us, was able to ignore many of the messages of his body-mind-spirit for a long time. This cultural inclination can be contrasted with ideas of the self that we see in other traditions, such as those expressed through contemplative practices, particularly Buddhism and yoga. In addition, I discuss the emergent paradigm prevalent in mind-body medicine, neuroscience, and related disciplines that acknowledges the inextricable relationships between mind and body, identifying some of the ways that such scientific inquiry can be supportive of healing justice and ways that it may limit the endeavor.

The chapter continues by introducing the healing justice framework and identifying each of the six dimensions of the self—the body, emotions, thoughts, spirit, community, and the natural world. Readers are also introduced to the six basic capabilities needed to attend to and care for these dimensions—mindfulness, compassion, curiosity, critical inquiry, effort, and equanimity. A more thorough explanation of these six capabilities is the subject of the next chapter.

Beyond the Mind-Body Split

It is easy to understand why one might be inclined to think of the body and mind as separate. Have you ever found yourself reading a whole page in a book (perhaps this one) and realized that you have no idea what you just read? The body was sitting there reading a book, and the mind was elsewhere (distracted or daydreaming), all of this perhaps pointing to the separateness of mind and body. Indeed, it is not uncommon for people to just think of themselves as a mind, a person who really only exists from the neck up. One may not even think about their body at all, unless it fails them, gets sick, or starts breaking down through aging. Why is it exactly that many people tend to favor a top-down approach to understanding and experiencing themselves rather than a bottom-up approach?

One explanation is that human brains have evolved such that thinking, conjuring, and planning, taking place in the prefrontal cortex that is unique to the species, is occurring almost nonstop, distracting us from actual felt and embodied experiences of the here and now.[1] While there is an evolutionary story to be told about this, I begin this discussion by directing attention to the origins of the so-called "mind-body split" in the Western philosophical traditions that inform culture, lives, and professions today.[2] The dualism of 17th-century philosopher Rene Descartes, actualized in his famous phrase, "I think therefore I am," asserts not only the distinctiveness of mind and body but privileges mind over body. Such a paradigm is further bolstered by a patriarchal culture that values the "rationality" of the mind (which the ancient Greek philosopher Aristotle associated with men) over the "irrationality" of the body (which he associated with women). In addition, the major Western patriarchal religions—Judaism, Islam, and Christianity—tend to take a view of the body as something sinful or something to be overcome or dominated. Moreover, Western, or allopathic, medicine, grounded in scientific empiricism, has been inclined to treat patients' bodies as machines rather than looking at the role that the mind (and social world) can play in health.[3] It is no wonder that giving compassionate attention to the whole self, and especially the body, is difficult for us, as it was for Stephan.

Given this context, it is not surprising that the theories and practices that drive social action, social services, and clinical work tend to perpetuate this mind-body split. The mind has been viewed as a rational mind, and other dimensions of consciousness have been ignored, in part because they have not been understood as scientifically observable.[4] Scientific empiricism and materialism have also restricted practitioner ability to fully understand the body, as understanding has been largely limited to observable behavior at best (e.g., body language that a therapist could observe). The gaze of Western clinical medicine has dulled human capacities for subjective internal awareness and experience of the body, known as *interoception*. The capability for interoception can play a significant role in healing and is an important capability both for the people practitioners work with, and themselves.[5–7]

Mensinga and others have noticed that the body historically has been conspicuously absent in the scholarship and practice of social work and related disciplines. Strengths perspective theorist Dennis Saleebey argued in 1992 that "the quality of both theory and practice had been compromised as a result of the profession's superficial attention to the body," despite a professed interest in the bio-psycho-social-spiritual person.[8]

Furthermore, teaching people how to cultivate an interoceptive relation-ship with the body (i.e., the ability to feel into what is going on internally) has been largely absent from the places where social practitioners are trained and educated—both in universities and in community-based set-tings. Fortunately, this situation is beginning to change—in the larger cul-ture, universities, and practice settings—toward deepening understanding of the mind-body connection.

The Mind-Body Connection

While indigenous, Eastern, and other traditions have long recognized the connections between the body and mind, it has only been in recent years that scholars and practitioners have recognized, theorized, and researched these connections. At a basic level, the mind-body connection is some-thing that everyone experiences all of the time—for example, when I think of a particular food I want to eat and my mouth waters, or when I have butterflies in my stomach when thinking about giving an important pres-entation to a group of people.[9] Or consider perhaps the effects that certain foods or drinks can have on one's state of mind (coffee anyone?).

Beyond this intuitive take on the mind-body connection, I explore two key knowledge domains that can inform understanding of the connection between the mind and body. The first is the insights from modern contem-plative and mind-body practices, particularly those that grew from a variety of Buddhist traditions (i.e., mindfulness) and those that grew out of clas-sical, hatha, and tantric yoga traditions (i.e., modern postural yoga). The second is the knowledge being developed in mind-body medicine (rooted in the previously noted traditions), including the role that mind-body prac-tices can play in alleviating stress, recovering from trauma, and preventing and treating illness. The knowledge base of mind-body medicine is sup-ported and complemented by research from neuroscience, evolutionary biology, neuropsychology, and psychoendocrinology, revealing powerful connections between the mind and the brain/body.

Introducing Modern Buddhist and Yogic Philosophy

Modern Buddhist philosophy and practice have been heavily influenced by Western ideas and intellectual movements such as the Enlightenment ideas of individualism, democratic political philosophy, and the ideas of romanticism and transcendentalism.[10] While these influences in how

Westerners understand Buddhism and, by extension, mindfulness, are strong, the various teachings of the Buddha have been central to the evolution of the philosophy and practices today. Modern Buddhism can be understood as based on the teachings of Gautama Buddha who lived around the sixth century BCE in the area around what is now Nepal. A tradition of oral and direct transmission, the classical Buddhist texts were not written until some 400 years after the life of the Buddha (whose name means "the awakened one").[11]

Modern Buddhist philosophical frameworks, grounded in subjective contemplative inquiry, teach that the mind and body are not two different things but are constituents of one organic process. The Buddha said: "If the body is not cultivated, the mind cannot be cultivated. If the body is cultivated then the mind can be cultivated."[12] To better understand this, imagine that you are watching a movie and something frightening happens; you may find yourself physically startled, perhaps causing you to jump in your seat or your heart rate to rise. This is an experience of the mind and body working as one. Indeed, when one tunes into one's experience of a particular emotion such as fear, one can actually feel the emotion in the body.

Also important is the role that the mind plays in how one experiences the world. The Buddha used the metaphor of the second arrow, teaching that there is the natural pain of getting shot by an arrow but that the human mind is inclined to create unnecessary suffering by conjuring a second arrow. This "second arrow" is the human thought processes that may go something like this—"Why me? Who shot the arrow? Why did he do it? I'm going to sue him," making the subjective experience of pain even worse. A famous quote attributed to the Buddha captures the power of the mind to influence human experience:

> The thought manifests as the word;
> The word manifests as the deed;
> The deed develops into habit;
> And habit hardens into character,
> So watch the thought and its ways with care,
> And let it spring from love
> Born out of concern for all beings.[13]

To "watch the thought and its ways with care" is a core activity of the practice of mindfulness. To be sure, thoughts are relational and contextual, and one's social location, including a history of and experience with marginalization or oppression will play a significant role in the process described in this quote.

Like Buddhism, modern yoga has been highly influenced by Western thought and practices, though it certainly originates, at least in part, from a variety of sources and strands of Indian religious thought and practice dating back thousands of years, some say to 3,000 BCE or before. The early texts of yoga that have been influential in the development of modern yoga, going back to the *Upanishads*, are thought to have been written prior to the common era, while the classic texts of yoga came later. While the *Bhagavad Gita*, composed between the fifth century BCE and second century CE, and the *Yoga Sutras*, estimated to have been written between the second century BCE and fourth century CE, are considered key texts that undergird the modern postural yoga movement, other texts such as those associated with Tantrism and hatha yoga have also been highly influential.[14]

When yoga eventually landed in the West, it was part of a countercultural spiritual movement, but today it is more often associated with body-based practices within the context of popular culture.[15] Many of the teachings of yoga have acknowledged the human tendency toward dualism and the suffering it causes. Thus, in terms of the inquiry into the mind-body connection, yoga (meaning "yoking") can be thought of as a practice of uniting the divide between the mind and body. While certainly some people enter into yoga thinking it will give them a better, more fit body, my belief is that people are streaming into yoga classes because of the culture of disembodiment and sense of dislocation, anxiety, and grief that it causes. According to the *Vijnana bhairava Tantra*, or *Radiance Sutras*, which first appeared as a written text around 800 AD:

> All around you, in every moment,
> The world is offering a feast for your senses.
> Songs are playing,
> Tasty food is on the table,
> Fragrances are in the air,
> Colors fill the eyes with light
> You who long for union,
> Attend this banquet with loving focus.
> The outer and inner worlds
> Open to each other.
> Oneness of vision, oneness of heart.

Right here, in the midst of it all,
Mount that elation, ascend with it,
Become identical
With the ecstatic essence
Embracing both worlds.[16]

Rather than overcoming or transcending the body and material world in the way that perhaps some of the early yogic texts espoused, one of the primary purposes of modern postural yoga, influenced by tantric traditions, is to learn to pay more attention to the body, to develop a relationship with it, and to cherish it deeply.

The practices of modern postural yoga (physical movements and breath practices done standing, sitting or lying down) invite a person to place their attention on a particular movement or experience. This may cause one to experience the mind and body in a more unified way, activating the "rest and digest" parasympathetic nervous system. Thus, the various practices of modern yoga—breathing, stretching, strengthening, and balancing—can serve to calm the mind.

From the perspective of these traditions, the apparent divide between mind and body is a false one and the practices can help one to overcome this delusion and experience more wholeness and connection. While a deep philosophical inquiry into the nuances of Buddhism and yoga is beyond the scope of this book, my purpose is to introduce you to other ways of understanding the relationship between body and mind, and to ground the practices of mindfulness and yoga that inform this book in their evolutionary contexts. This book continues this exploration, inviting you into an inquiry into your own self and helping you to develop the necessary skills to apply the practices of wholeness and connection to your life and work.

Mind-Body Medicine and Neuroscience

Mind-body medicine has been described as a "collection of treatments that recognize the bidirectional nature of psyche and soma."[17] It emphasizes the internal capacities or strengths that humans have to heal themselves. To take advantage of the potential benefits (subjective or otherwise) of mind-body medicine does not mean that one should not seek out medicines, surgeries, or other Western scientifically based assessments and interventions when one needs them. Indeed, integrative medicine seeks to integrate both Western and mind-body medicine together. What is unique about mind-body medicine is that it recognizes the innate capacity of the human mind to aid people in reducing stress and helping them to return to homeostasis. Two corollary concepts may be helpful here too. One is functional medicine, which is concerned with the underlying causes of disease (as opposed to just symptoms); and the other is holistic medicine, which views disease as an imbalance in the whole system.[18] Such approaches are resonant with and informed by traditional approaches to medicine including homeopathy, Chinese medicine, and Ayurveda, the traditional medicine of India.

The corpus of evidence relevant to mind-body medicine has been growing exponentially in recent years. Herbert Benson, who coined the term "relaxation response," was the first researcher, in the 1960s and 1970s, to study the impact of transcendental meditation on the body, specifically measuring blood pressure.[19] Today, there are literally thousands of research articles focusing on a range of interventions, including biofeedback, loving-kindness meditation, progressive muscle relaxation, transcendental meditation, mindfulness meditation, yoga, hypnosis, and integrative restoration (iRest), to alleviate an even broader range of conditions, such as asthma, cancer, high blood pressure, obesity, diabetes, fibromyalgia, depression, posttraumatic stress disorder, and anxiety.[20] Though this research is promising, there are also many legitimate concerns about it. For example, there are plenty of other studies that reveal inconclusive results about the impact of mindfulness on various outcomes including positive mood, attention, and recovery from substance abuse, to name a few, and about whether meditation was a better intervention than other ones.[21] As well, most studies on yoga, mindfulness, and similar practices focus only on the short term, so the scientific community does not know much about what the long-term impacts are, at least from a research perspective.

The findings of neuropsychology and related disciplines have been helpful in pointing to a connection between the mind and the brain/body.[22] Scientists are showing that the mind, including every random thought one ever has, shapes the brain, creating new neural pathways and reinforcing old ones. One of the more powerful findings of neuroscience can be explained by the concept of neuroplasticity, which essentially affirms that the brain, which the scientific community once thought was finished developing at around age 25, can actually change. Practices such as meditation have been shown, through the use of such measurement tools as magnetic resonance imaging, that the gray matter of the brain actually changes when one meditates.

Another example of the role of the brain and body in mind processes relates to how one responds to stressful situations, an adaptive function from human evolutionary development, stemming from the times when humans were constantly seeking to avoid dangerous or lethal threats. When humans are under threat or stress, whether it is acute (state anxiety) or chronic (trait anxiety), the sympathetic nervous systems are activated and stress hormones are released throughout the body.[23] This "fight or flight" response activates a cascade of neurological events beginning in the amygdala, sending an alarm to be on alert. At the same time, cortisol is released by the adrenal glands, essentially overriding many of the brain's higher functions and suppressing the immune system to reduce potential inflammation that could occur in the threatening situation.[24] Clearly, an experience of the mind such as fear has an associated physical process.

Despite these rich findings, there are important critiques of the neuroscience research to be made as well. One of the problems that is particularly useful to explore, and especially relevant to a healing justice perspective, is that when the mind is equated with the brain, scientists are ignoring the fact that the mind includes the whole embodied being in relation to others.[25] Humans get input from the world around them, and they process those experiences using a shared social language. The zeitgeist of the research community's fixation on the study of the brain and the idea that attention or some other aspect of mindfulness is located in the brain arguably perpetuates not only scientific materialism but also isolation and narcissism so prevalent in the culture. Beth Berila has offered her perspective on this issue:

> Like the recent trend in scientific research on the impact of meditation on the brain, we can value and learn from that work but we also need to deeply critique the sudden "credibility" given to ancient traditions or to feminist work once Eurocentric and patriarchal science steps in. While we can learn deeply from the important and valuable scientific work being done, feminists have long been skeptical of the ways science has historically been used to discredit traditional ways of knowing.[26]

The political project of healing justice is to reclaim the parts of the self that not only have been silenced but to strengthen capabilities to feel, know, and understand the whole self through a variety of ways of knowing. This reclamation of inherent human wisdom, including the practice wisdom of social workers, counselors, and activists, what has been called "guilty knowledge," is an act of resistance to patriarchy, colonization, capitalism, White supremacy, and ableism.[27] Social work scholar and citizen of the Arikara (Sahnish) and Hidatsa Nations Michael Yellowbird has used the term "neurodecolonization" to describe this reclamation, building on the acumen of neuroscientists and affirming that mindfulness and traditional ceremonies can "train the mind and change the brain's capacity to heal from the trauma of colonialism."[28]

Expanding the Field: The Whole Self

Going deeper into an inquiry into who humans are, in an effort to better understand the need for and the best ways to take care of and heal oneself, I now expand the paradigm of the mind-body to a concept that already exists in literature on social work practice, namely the *bio-psycho-social-spiritual* person.[29] This is a useful framework because it allows one to incorporate the body (*bio*), and the mind (*psycho*), including both the cognitive and affective dimensions into the inquiry. In addition, it expands the field to include explicitly the spiritual or transpersonal dimension of the self (*spiritual*), as well as that dimension of the self affected by, and which cocreates, social, political, cultural, and economic relationships and systems (*social*). Thus caring for oneself fully and completely, and in a transformative way, asks one to attend to all of these dimensions.

The Ecological Self

Here I trouble the waters a bit by exploring this great philosophical question of "the self." The answer I offer will not fully satisfy metaphysicians, but the inquiry is salient and necessary for a holistic and transformational approach to self-care. The question of the whole self is important and relevant to the possibilities of healing and transformation of people and communities, including oneself, particularly in a culture that tends to be more individually oriented and disconnected from nature and spirit. The philosophical position, known by environmental thinkers as "deep ecology," offers a different and perhaps useful perspective on the self.[30] The growing body of evidence from neuroscience and related disciplines can also support this exploration of the ecological self. Discussion of the ecological self is especially relevant in the era of what some geologists and environmental advocates are calling the anthropocene, a geological period whereby human activity is so prevalent as to impact biodiversity and the climate.

Ostensibly, humans are all separate beings, distinct from one another in physical bodies and psycho-spiritual selves. One naturally goes through an individuation process as one moves from infancy to adulthood. Indeed, the parietal lobes of the brain establish this sense of separation from the world.[31] This "skin encapsulated ego," as Alan Watts called it, can also be considered a metaphorical construct that can serve one well in their abilities to survive and fulfill self-interests.[32] From a human rights perspective, this sense of individuality implies a normative claim that every individual on the planet can actualize his or her self-agency, as well as feel safe from being harmed by others. From the perspective of deep ecology though, which views all things (plants, animals, the air, the sun, the trees, dirt, humans, etc.) as interconnected, the Western, modernist idea of the self is limited and problematic. Gregory Bateson referred to this conventional notion of the self as one of "the epistemological fallacies of Occidental civilization."[33] The deep ecological self, however, is a superlative expanded self, and it includes everything; in fact, it is not really a "thing" per se but more of a process.

For many cultures that are more collectively oriented, the Westerner's concern with individuating the self is almost incomprehensible, a construction that is indistinguishable from family, community, nature, or divine forces. Eco-feminists have also offered similar positions.[34] Similarly, quantum physicists have shown that the Newtonian idea that the world is made up of separate objects that collide is highly problematic.[35] Instead, one might consider the idea that everything is interconnected and microprocesses happening in one's body right now are, perhaps imperceptibly, connected to processes happening in near and far parts of the universe. Humans are constantly exchanging matter and energy with their environment; as Rick Hanson has noted, "the apparent wall between your body and the world is more like a picket fence."[36]

And so the journey of self-care is not just about ourselves. Deep ecologist Arne Naess uses the term "self-realization" to describe a progression where the self to be realized is widened and includes more and more of the world. This kind of human developmental framework has some resonance with integral theory, which affirms a developmental process that moves progressively toward the transpersonal.[37] Thus this "ecological self" recognizes that "this place is part of myself."[38] Stephan was tuned into just such an intuition, feeling that his life was about more than the needs of his skin-encapsulated ego but that he was called to merge his needs with those of the world around him.

The Buddhist philosophical term "dependent arising," as it has been interpreted by modern thinkers, resonates with this worldview of deep ecology. Dependent arising means that nothing exists or arises out of nothing; everything is always coming into being based on specific causes, conditions, and contingencies.[39] I exist in this moment in a particular way because of my parents coming together at a specific time and place, because of the sun and rain and people that have grown the food that has nourished my body, because of the myriad choices I and others have made, because of the interactions with others that have led me here, ad infinitum.

These perspectives can lead one to the idea that perhaps a sense of place is part of who we are. When people are displaced from their geographies, they are not the same people as they were in their natural settings. There are countless cases throughout history where people's identities are forever changed due to displacement from their locale—for example, when the Norwegian government facilitated the movement of indigenous people from the Arctic coast to interior urban areas of Norway, or when public officials flew hurricane survivors from urban New Orleans to places like rural Utah, or when Hmong refugees from the mountains of Vietnam were resettled in the United States after the Vietnam War.[40] In her book *Root Shock*, Mindy Fullilove describes the stories of displacement in US cities like Roanoke, Virginia, and Pittsburgh, Pennsylvania, a result of housing policies, disinvestment, gentrification, and mass incarceration.[41] Drawing from her insights about gardening and the experience that a plant goes through when it is uprooted and replanted, she notes the effects of displacement on the minds, bodies, spirits, and communities of mostly African Americans. Her thesis confirms the human connection to place. She writes,

> Because we dance in a ballroom, have a parade in the street, make love in a bedroom, and prepare a feast in a kitchen, each of these places becomes imbued with sounds, smells, noises, and feelings of those moments and how we lived them. . . . The cues from place dive under conscious thought, and awaken our sinews and bones, where days of our lives have been recorded.[42]

Thus context matters to not only one's identity, but it is intricately connected to other parts of the self, including the body, mind, community, and spirit.

In the social work field, practitioners use a framework known as "the person-in-environment." In this framework, a person is necessarily a part of his or her surroundings; one can never be separate from the social systems, culture, families, and language that play roles in constructing who a person is. However, the field has primarily emphasized the social dimension of environment and given only scant attention to geographies and ecologies.[43] Of course, sometimes, it is necessary for the focus to stay on the individual, but it is always a construct, and one can never really be separated from one's ecology. All of this is to say that healing justice implies that practitioners attend to the deepest and most expansive definition of the self.

A book about self-care could easily perpetuate a problem that is evident in self-care and personal growth communities, namely a culture of narcissism. In particular, spiritual practitioners who identify as people of color or queer have noted the ways that the dominant worldview of White, middle-class, heteronormativity is perpetuated in such settings (e.g., in yoga studios).[44] People can become completely obsessed with their own wellbeing (the health of their bodies, the state of their emotions, their spiritual progress, etc.) and forget that their welfare is inextricably linked with the health of the wetlands outside of their town, or with the family in a neighborhood in another part of their city, or with a social movement on another continent.

While there has always been human suffering, one could argue that much of the stress that people experience in their lives today may be better understood as an embodiment of the pain of the earth rather than as an individual pathology. According to psychotherapist Miriam Greenspan,

> Our bodies, hearts, and souls carry the news of our endangered earth. Our emotions, when we allow them to, bring the earth's cries to us. Because we are all interconnected in the web of life, and because that web is poisoned and threatened, the wounds of the earth are our wounds. We carry them in ways that we don't necessarily recognize or connect to the state of the earth. But if we listen, we can feel the earth's voice within us. We are called to listen.[45]

Our fates are linked. From this perspective, I can never be whole and free as long as the earth and the people on it feel fractured and oppressed. I think this insight implies two things. First, we must take care of ourselves, each other, and the earth for real transformation to occur. Second, since we are all in this together, we do not have to be too preoccupied with

self improvement, uptight, or in a big hurry for our personal transformation, because if you look inside and around you might notice that we all
have a long way to go.

A Framework for Healing Justice

It is often skillful to narrow one's focus of care onto one's own little piece
of the universe. This is especially necessary for people who have had a
tendency to take care of others before taking care of themselves. This may
be particularly true for women, people who are marginalized in society or
culturally conditioned to be caretakers of those with privilege, people with
a history of codependent relationships, and people in the helping professions. But, when it is skillful, one can expand the lens of the self to include
the wider field. So healing justice may mean a lot of different things—
acknowledging and forgiving yourself when you make a mistake, staying
home from work when you feel a cold coming on, going on a walk during
lunch hour, nurturing a relationship with a friend, standing in solidarity
with those who are targeted by draconian social policies, or organizing
coworkers to create better working conditions.

Each chapter of Part II of this book will develop more fully holistic self-
care practices associated with each of the areas of the self—the body, the
mind-heart, spirit, community, and nature. I consider these dimensions
of the self separately, for the purpose of learning and inquiry, as well as
for effective action. But, clearly, the premise of the book is that each of the
dimensions is mutually reinforcing the other and is a construct.

Grounded in the preceding analysis and my own journey of transformative practice, Figure 3.1 reveals the healing justice framework as a visual
diagram, offering a map for the journey of healing justice. Toward the center of the diagram, there are the three core dimensions of the self that one
is called to care for—the body, emotions, and thoughts. Later, I refer to the
latter two combined as the mind-heart. These three core dimensions of the
self are informed by and are manifested through three other dimensions
of the self. The first dimension is community, which is the social connections one has, including families, neighborhoods, language, social institutions, cultural practices, economic systems, and so on. The second is
nature, which is the nonhuman elements (wind, grass, trees, tigers, fleas,
etc.), including the stuff humans build out of these elements (houses,
chairs, cars, coffee cups, etc.) and the processes of the earth, the solar
system, and beyond (change of seasons, moon phases, photosynthesis,

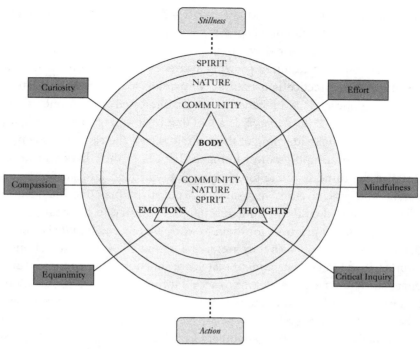

FIGURE 3.1 Healing Justice Framework

natural ecologies, etc.). The third of these other dimensions is spirit, the transpersonal dimension of the self, which includes nonmaterial, energetic, or divine forces in the self or world. Notice that these three other dimensions appear twice—creating, supporting, and informing a person from both the inside and outside. They have such a profound impact on who a person is, and yet the dominant culture conditions people to ignore them when thinking about who they are. Thus these six dimensions of the whole self are what we are concerned with caring for, restoring, and, if needed, transforming. The outer circles are the capabilities that support the ongoing practice and inquiry of healing justice.

The six capabilities that can facilitate healing and transformation are mindfulness and compassion, curiosity and critical inquiry, and equanimity and effort. The next chapter is devoted to developing these ideas more fully and explaining their importance for healing justice. Here I offer a very brief definition of each one. *Mindfulness* is a simple concept, though not exactly easy to do all the time, but it just means to intentionally practice being present with and noticing what is happening in the moment. The approach of this book is to develop such presence with the whole self.[46] *Compassion* is an essential support for mindfulness. As one cultivates awareness of who one is or what is happening, it only works when one does it in a kindhearted way, relinquishing self-judgment. The cultivation of *curiosity* toward one's growing awareness of themselves and their healing justice practice is a natural companion to compassion. Instead of judging oneself, the invitation is to get interested in who one is and what one needs. *Critical inquiry* is a tool that invites practitioners to learn about the habitual patterning of their whole selves, the causes and consequences, cultivating the power to make changes in their lives and work. Because the mind is prone to checking out—through fantasizing, social media, and psychic numbing—and to a negativity bias one must make *effort*, and indeed cultivate some discipline, to engage in the healing justice inquiries and practices for them to work. Finally, *equanimity* is a practice of accepting things as they are; it is a letting go of the fruits of one's efforts with a kind of detachment that is not cold but rather connected and engaged. When people endeavor to accept things as they are, it puts them in a more powerful position to make changes when needed—in self, with others, and in social systems. While there is a prevalent assumption that detachment means disengagement or lack of caring, it just means that one creates a little space between one's agendas and themselves.

Finally, the diagram contains a pole that runs through the center, with stillness at one end and action at the other end. The purpose of these two orientations is twofold. First, they represent the techniques of inquiring into or checking in with the whole self, either from a place of stillness (e.g., when meditating or lying in bed at night reflecting on the day) or from a place of action (e.g., walking in nature or while working with a client). Both are necessary to further people's understanding of who they are and what is happening in any given moment and cultivating their ability to discern what they, and others, may need.

Second, the poles are concerned with how to respond to what is happening as one inquires into the truth of the matter using any combination of the six lenses of the self. One may choose just to notice and to stay still, to do nothing about it. One may choose to stay with what is, even if it is an uncomfortable experience or insight. In some situations, staying with *what is* actually happening can invite transformation, teaching someone not to run from or fight with what they do not like. According to Buddhist teacher Pema Chodron, "It's a transformative experience to simply pause instead of immediately filling up the space. By waiting, we begin to connect with fundamental restlessness as well as fundamental spaciousness."[47] If you notice a wave of anger coming over you, perhaps you are able to just notice any sense of warmth or contraction in the body, or the thoughts that come along with it, and choose not to act on the anger, by telling someone off or firing out an e-mail you may regret later. On the action end, as a result of mindful observations and insights that arise, one can tune into the choices that are available in terms of action (though consciously not taking action is perhaps a kind of action too). It may be more skillful to choose to take action, to alleviate one's own suffering (or others') in the moment, bringing one into balance. A very simple example is that if you notice you are hungry and haven't eaten for a while, then you eat. Throughout the book, I explore and develop the discernment and skillful means needed for this kind of healing justice practice.

Putting It Into Practice
Inquiry

Find a comfortable place to sit or lie down where you can close your eyes. Notice the places where your body is touching the furniture or ground and allow yourself to feel the connection. Take a couple of deep breaths. Now think about a time, recently or in the past, where you felt happy/joyful or when you found something funny. Allow yourself to really feel it. Where do you feel it in your body? What is the shape, color, and texture of it? Stay connected to the feeling in your body as long as you can, perhaps watching it dissipate. When it has dissolved, take a deep breath, open your eyes, and/ or sit up. How would you describe the experience you had of noticing this kind of emotion in the body? If you didn't notice anything, what was that like? Reflect on how often you feel your emotions in the body. What does this mean to you in terms of the implications for a self-care practice of the mind-body or whole self?

Self-Care Practice Skill

This is an introduction to the practice of mindful eating. I talk about this skill in more detail later in the chapter on the body, but you are invited here to engage in a basic eating meditation. Find something to eat or drink that you enjoy, perhaps a snack like a piece of fruit or chips that you can eat with your hands, or a cup of juice or tea. Sitting at a table or on the floor, set the item in front of you and take two deep breaths as you look at the item, really taking it in with your eyes. Then, take another deep breath. Begin to reflect on how the food or drink you have chosen got to you. Consider its journey to you and think about the processes it went through along the way, from its time growing in the ground, to harvesting and processing, and transportation. Think about the roles of the sun and the rain and the people who were involved in helping it on its journey to the store you got it from.

Now take another deep breath. Put the item in your hand and notice what it feels like in your hand, the warmth of a cup or the feeling of the food touching your hand. Take a bite or a sip. What do you notice? Do that two more times (i.e., two more bites or two more drinks) in your own time, noticing the textures and tastes in your mouth. Now you are done with the meditation and you can just finish your snack or drink in your usual way (assuming this was not your usual way). Reflect on what you learned.

Experiment for a Day

For one day, you are invited to engage in a practice called "noticing connection." This is an opportunity for you to begin to take stock (nonjudgmentally) of the times throughout your day and evening when you feel connected or not—with yourself, others, and/or your environment. You are not being asked to engage in a formal mindfulness practice per se; you are only being asked to notice the times when you feel tuned in, a sense of belonging, or just a sense of being alive. It may not be as profound as when Stephan was touching the dirt, it might just be an ordinary experience of connection, like feeling the warmth of a sweater on your skin. Likewise, you are asked to notice times when you might feel checked out, a lack of belonging, or disconnected from your life.

On a piece of paper, make two columns and write "connection" and "disconnection" on each side. Then create six rows along the left-hand side, one for each dimension of your whole self—Body, Emotions, Thoughts, Community, Nature, and Spirit. Jot down anything you experience throughout the day in the appropriate category. You may write about what you noticed, such as feeling the warm water on your skin in the shower (Body/ Connection), or feeling isolated from your colleagues during a workplace birthday party (Community/Disconnection). You may also want to check and see if specific adjectives or feeling descriptors come up for you in relation to the noticing ("felt pleasurable"; "felt like I didn't belong with my workmates"). You may find that you only notice a few of the categories and that you do not have any noticings in some categories at all. That is okay, the point for now is just to see what you might notice and begin to learn about the framework. Don't worry if you can't figure out what category something is in; they often cross over, of course. This is just an opportunity to begin learning about what these dimensions of the whole self mean to you and to learn what it feels like for you personally to experience "connection" and "disconnection."

A Skillful Path of Healing Justice

*"We have to face the pain we have been running from. In
fact, we need to learn to rest in it and let its searing power
transform us."*

—CHARLOTTE JOKO BECK[1]

Case Study

*Jacky was a therapist at a social services agency that served adults and youth sur-
viving family violence. She was both a survivor of childhood sexual assault and a
formerly battered woman herself. Her personal experience, as well as her feminist
sensibility, called her to advocate for and protect women and children; she was
deeply committed to helping them heal from the trauma they experienced. After
her divorce, as a single parent, she pursued her counseling degree, completing it
when she was 43 years old. Since then, she has worked at the same agency for eight
years and hopes to work there until retirement.*

*Jacky was satisfied with her work and was a faithful employee, arriving at
8:00 AM every morning and heading out at 4:30 PM sharp, only leaving early
occasionally for a doctor's appointment or to pick up her children from school
or activities. She had a boy, Zach, 14, and a girl, Rebecca, 12, from her previous
marriage. Her new partner, Natalie, who is a co-parent to the kids, has been a tremendous source of support in her life and work. She also found support in a local
LGBTQ community organization through her volunteer position as the treasurer
of the board of directors.*

*Jacky was always the first employee to turn in her paperwork at the end of
each month, dotting all the "i's" and crossing all the "t's" in her case notes and
grant reports. She believed in maintaining firm boundaries between herself and
clients and was known in the office for being very rigid; she would refuse to see
clients if they were late and often called coworkers out on what she believed to be*

unprofessional behavior. She was strict with her children, and only a minority of clients felt much of a connection to her. Her modus operandi was "control, control, control." She controlled her schedule and her feelings and asserted too much control in the therapeutic process with clients. While Jacky was a compassionate person and had much to offer, the fact of the matter was that being around Jacky was kind of a bummer, including for Jacky.

One day she received the devastating news that a neighbor was trying to molest her daughter, Rebecca. The father of a child that Rebecca had been babysitting had been making inappropriate comments for several weeks and that afternoon he had attempted to touch her daughter; fortunately, Rebecca told him to "go to hell" and ran out of the house. Natalie was at home when Rebecca came running through the door and disclosed what had happened. When Jacky found out about it when she got home from work, she went into crisis intervention mode trying to comfort her daughter, going to the neighbor's house, calling the authorities, and doing anything she could think of to help. While Rebecca was shaken, she was actually doing okay. Everyone knew she was lucky to have been able to leave the scene and tell her family about it before she was seriously hurt. With continued support, she was sure to recover from the experience.

But that night as Jacky lay in bed, not sleeping, she broke apart. This horrible thing had happened to her child and though it could have been much worse, she had tried with every fiber of her being to prevent it. Something painful had happened that had been out of her control. She felt like a terrible parent and person and that she had failed miserably. And, if controlling herself, the world, and the people around her didn't prevent pain, then what did? And who exactly was she if she wasn't controlling everything?

While her daughter insisted on going to school the next day, Jacky stayed home from work. She felt broken and lost, and continued to use several sick days, not knowing what to do with herself. On the weekend, Natalie suggested that they go to a drumming circle at the LGBTQ center, and Jacky, feeling like she had nothing to lose, decided to join her. As she picked up a drum and started playing along with others, she felt kind of awkward. But, the drumming slowly began to penetrate her being—from without and within. She could feel the emotions releasing out of her—anger, shame, grief. She noticed that her thoughts, usually racing, were still. She continued to throw her whole self into the drumming, her sense of self expanding. She looked around at the people she was playing with and felt embraced by them. When the evening was over, she felt a sense of peace, wholeness, and calm, beneath the waves of pain and troubles.

As they drove home that night, Jacky's problems were still before her—her neighbor, her daughter, her family, her unresolved past. She knew she had serious issues as a result of the past and that she wanted to let go of her tendency to try and control everything. She didn't know how, but even that didn't matter. She acknowledged all of this to Natalie and realized her need to control had been a natural response to her past experiences. In the face of all of this though, she felt hopeful.

Jacky began to attend the drumming sessions regularly. She bought her own drums and even started playing at home, getting the whole family involved and hosting circles at the house. It was therapeutic, and it began to soften her. At some level, she was still "responsible Jacky," who had control issues. But she was able to create a little distance with that person, laugh at herself a bit, have more compassion for herself and others, and loosen up her rigidity. She was learning to let go of her attachments to schedule and structure and was allowing others to do the same. She became more comfortable in her own skin, and those around her appreciated her more. She is now working on a certificate in music therapy and hopes to incorporate it into her current work with clients or find a new job where she can.

Introduction

There is a famous book by Buddhist teacher Pema Chodron called *When Things Fall Apart*.[2] She teaches that in such situations, transformation can become possible when one can acknowledge that one has hit rock bottom, lean into and learn about difficult emotions, even let them blow one over, and eventually stand up and go forward. Crisis situations can upset the applecart of one's general state. For most people, a general state is avoidance of what is really going on, "spending our whole lives escaping from the monsters of our minds."[3] People avoid their realities through endless distractions, addictions, and like the case of Jacky, by trying to control their own and others' lives. For her, learning about the potential victimization of her daughter, caused her world to fall apart. But it created an opportunity to touch into the suffering that she had been working so hard to avoid for many years. By bravely joining her community that night for drumming, she was able to step into the messy, painful, and beautiful reality of her human life and find powers in herself that she didn't know she had. It would eventually allow her to be more capable to offer the same to her clients.

In this chapter, I explore more deeply the human predicament and the ways that minds, culture, and social systems can create suffering, disconnecting one from the whole self, one's deepest passions for life, and the people one works with. This discussion segues into a skillful path of change for healing justice practice, which one might think of as a lifelong process of slowly peeling away the layers of an onion. Through this conversation, I begin to move toward a discussion of healing justice as a practice journey that can alleviate and indeed transform suffering and allow practitioners to live to their fullest potentials in their lives and work. A central theme of the path is balance, between the extremes of trying to control one's life and work, on the one hand, and letting things be, on the other. I then move into a deeper discussion of the six capabilities for healing justice—mindfulness and compassion, curiosity and critical inquiry, and equanimity and effort, which were introduced in the previous chapter. The chapter concludes by sharing a powerful, evidence-based practice called nurturing the positive, which can be a useful source of support going forward.

The Human Predicament and the Whole Self

According to many contemplative traditions, human beings suffer because they are ignorant of their true natures. The Sanskrit word *avidya* means spiritual ignorance and in the yogic tradition implies an inability to see things clearly, as they really are, especially oneself.[4] People tend to identify with the egoic self, which consists of a conglomeration of the body, thoughts, feelings, and experiences. Neuropsycholgists have noted that this self gets played out in "the simulator," the place in the mind where the movie that each person is producing, directing, and starring in is projected.[5] Similarly, a concept from the psychotherapeutic tradition, the false self, means that everyone has a façade that they present to the world and that they tend to identify with.[6,7] Originating in psychoanalytic theory, the idea is that the false self emerges from failures in the mothering relationship, though it is appropriate to expand the causes for the emergence of the false self to include various aspects of Western culture, a harsh capitalist economy, and social systems of oppression. In the end, these delusions keep a person endlessly distracted from knowing and embodying what might be thought of as a more authentic self.

Of course, everyone needs a sense of self as they learn to function in the world; it gives a person boundaries, identity, and meaning in relation to others and the world around them. For people who are marginalized and whose identities may tend to be silenced or attacked in the dominant culture, asserting a sense of identity, sometimes in strategic solidarity with like others, is essential for survival and is an expression of the authentic self. But when one is caught up in the small, disconnected false self and its misguided storylines, one may miss a sense of connection to a greater whole and forget about the authentic self that Jacky discovered, one that has the possibility to be experienced as spacious, connected, and spontaneous. This narrowness of self plays out in the discourse, policies, and practices of "us" versus "them" that transpires between neighborhoods, political parties, and countries.

Author Jeremy Rifkin has explored how empathy for others (tribes, cultures, and now global humanity) has developed over time.[8] He believes that the globalizing world is inviting people toward a new evolution of empathy, what he calls an empathic sociability, or an empathic civilization.[9] While the mind did evolve for separation, the world we are living in today is perhaps now asking us to remember what Tibetan Buddhist teacher Chogyam Trungpa called "basic goodness,"[10] something that everyone naturally possesses. We can move beyond a sense of separation toward what deep ecologists call self-realization, or the evolution of the ecological self.[11] While many people may be willing to do this with others who are pretty much like them already—people one works with or shares political views with—one of the great challenges of the times appears to be to develop this empathy and understanding for people with whom we don't share values or class or ethnicity, or who we may even view as an enemy. For some people, healing justice may mean developing the capacities to do this kind of work, through intergroup dialogue and courageous social justice conversations. Of course, people need to feel safe from any threat of violence be able to readily engage in such processes, as well as to have done a certain amount of healing from their own oppression and trauma.

This idea of fundamental goodness is a departure from many of the viewpoints that have informed Western culture, which is influenced by the Christian doctrine of original sin. This position states that humans are ethically depraved and are powerless to rehabilitate themselves without an outside intervention or savior. Similarly, the secular religion of capitalism teaches that people are not enough and that what they need are larger homes, more fashionable clothes, and shinier techno-gadgets, all of which are contingent and fleeting. Fundamental goodness suggests that you are already okay just as you are.

In Buddhist philosophy, *avidya* or *ignorance* (i.e., delusion, confusion, and bewilderment) of one's authentic self can be understood as one of the primary causes of suffering. This ignorance is one of the three unwholesome roots of the mind, along with *attachment* (i.e., clinging to what is pleasant, or greed) and *aversion* (i.e., avoiding what is unpleasant, or hatred).[12] Ignorance, from this perspective, rests in the misapprehension of the ego or self, the false assumption that it is solid and unchanging and that humans are separate from one other. It is a failure to understand that humans are not just their thoughts and feelings, or bodies but are whole, interconnected beings.

Many of my students identify as internally wounded from painful and unprocessed experiences and feel some level of disengagement from their bodies, emotions, each other, and the natural world. This situation zaps vital energy and can disconnect them from their personal and collective power that could otherwise be unleashed for social change. For people living with trauma or who experience ongoing marginalization, as well as for people working with those who are, this kind of fracturedness can be acute, as was the case in Jacky's life. Many people particularly experience this sense of disembodiment or disconnection in terms of the basic visceral experiences of being in a human body, whether it is the sensations of feeling tired or sad or the pleasures associated with relaxing or tasting.

The capability to be interoceptive—to feel, know, and even appreciate the wisdom of one's body—has been hijacked by a host of aggressive cultural and social forces, from the global racism against brown bodies to the disconnected gaze of the physician, creating a near constant state of anxiety for some people. In Western culture, we tend to add to this disconnection and confusion by insulating ourselves from nature and the cycles of the seasons, as we pillage the earth for fossil fuels and sit indoors in the air conditioning during the summer. Many people today may find themselves preferring to communicate through social media or texting rather than looking someone in the eyes and having a conversation.

To cope with this predicament of disconnection from one's more authentic self, human minds are busy desperately grasping at something that could make them feel better or help them figure out their existential predicament. Recall that neuroscience teaches that brains are hardwired for avoidance and attachment, obsessive thinking, and a negativity bias.[13] Thus today people may become obsessive about cell phones, exercise programs, level of coffee consumption, and how, if only one's controlling boss would leave one alone, everything would be okay. Some people waver between trying too hard/being too rigid in their attempts to relieve stress at one extreme or giving up too easily/feeling defeated to the point that there is no point in trying at all at the other extreme. At the center of all this mess is a strong sense of self-judgment, as people's critical internal dialogue with themselves sabotages their best efforts. This ignorant, grasping, and aversive mind is like, as the Indian sage Ramana Maharshi said, "a drunken monkey being stung by scorpions."

Understandably, people deal with these painful circumstances by numbing themselves with intoxicants, technology, work, shopping, food, television, and entertainment. For some people the idea of self-care translates into a weekend marathon of chicken wings and a whole season of an HBO drama. While there is no need to feel ashamed for such behavior, such an approach is perhaps better termed self-indulgence. For others, self-care is a dirty word that implies selfishness or neoliberal narcissism. Perhaps all of these perspectives have succumbed to the fallacy of self-denial. Being hooked by this fallacy can render practitioners disconnected from their deepest, compassionate selves and their own intuition. This intuition is essential for social practitioners who are trying to offer something of value to their communities, as opposed to perpetuating and projecting individual and collective neuroses. It is when one has the opportunity to begin to reconnect with the wisdom of the whole self that one can start to have greater access to one's intuition. As such, practitioners can come to learn what they might really need in any given moment, connect to their personal and collective power, and in turn act effectively, on behalf of themselves and the communities they are part of.

Healing justice practice offers an antidote to this predicament we are all in together. Through the practices, there is an opportunity to reclaim human connections with each other and oneself. These practices are the focus of both Part II and Part III of the book, but as a teaser, one example of a practice to facilitate this connection is known as integral restoration, or iRest. While the evidence base is new, this modality has already been shown to be effective in a few studies.[14] iRest is a form of practice called *yoga nidra*, or the "yoga of sleep" and offers guided meditations to help people "rediscover their essential wholeness and their interconnectedness with all of life."[15] It is a gentle practice that is accessible to anyone, including those who have experienced trauma, and is traditionally done lying down on the floor (or bed or couch) but can be done sitting up too. It begins with progressive muscle relaxation, then takes the participant on a guided journey that creates an opportunity for discernment between the small self and a larger, more expansive sense of self. Research reveals a variety of positive outcomes, including stress reduction, better sleep, alleviation of posttraumatic stress disorder symptoms for trauma victims, and more mindfulness. Qualitative findings point to more acceptance of life's circumstances and more confidence in one's capacity to make choices. There are excellent yoga nidra and iRest guided meditations available on the Internet that may be helpful for anyone interested in this kind of practice. Given these potential outcomes, consider the impact that this could have on the ability of practitioners and the people they work with to function more effectively. The sense of integration is an ideal antidote to the sense of fracturedness and disconnectedness I have discussed throughout this chapter.

A Skillful Path of Change

The Sanskrit word *samskara* means "groove" or "impression," and it refers to the habitual patterns that are present in the mind-body, and indeed whole self, continuum. For example, coming home after work every night and having a glass of red wine creates a *samskara* in a person. It is a habitual pattern (not necessarily good or bad) that, once solidified through repetition, can be difficult to change. Even though the action may change, the impression is still there and pretty much impossible to ever completely really get rid of. A *samskara* can be understood as the equivalent of the neurological pathways that are being studied by scientists today. One can also think of these patterns as having physical, cognitive, emotional, social, and energetic dimensions. This is why making real change is much more complex than a behaviorist might have one believe. Rather than just changing one's actions, consciousness itself must be changed, and this includes addressing not only the physical and emotional dimensions of the behavior but also the cognitive beliefs that support the habit, such as "I am a stressed-out kind of person and red wine is the only thing that relieves me." To be sure, such individual behavioral patterns are most certainly influenced by other dimensions of the self as well; that is, spirit, community, and nature, as family, culture, and context all prefigure into the development of one's neural pathways.

The body is a critical and accessible site for learning about such patterning, and it is intricately connected to the other aspects of the whole self. Meditation teacher Eckhart Tolle refers to the human body as the "pain-body."[16] The pain-body, he writes, contains the emotional energy that gets stuck in the physical body, as unprocessed experiences leave a residue in the cells and energetic field. This means that if someone who was chronically overweight lost weight just by eating less and exercising more, they would most likely gain it all back eventually because they have not addressed the complexity of energy, thoughts, and samskaras beneath the surface. St. Thomas wrote over 2,000 years ago in *The Gnostic Gospels*: "If you bring forth that which is within you, that which you bring forth will save you. If you do not bring forth that which is within you, that which you do not bring forth will destroy you." Thus embarking on a healing justice journey implies attention to one's multidimensionality and the unseen realms of the psychospiritual field. It is a patient, even lifelong, process that is like unraveling the knots in a tangled cord or hose.

I believed for a long time that my body was something to be conquered, to be chipped away at. For example, I have carried excess weight on and off over the years, and it was something I didn't like about myself, so I had to figure out how to get rid of it. I engaged in excessive exercise to the point of hurting myself and dieting to the point of depriving myself. I tried to figure out this riddle in my conceptual mind and came to the misguided conclusion that the solution had to be about willpower and overcoming desire. Fortunately, I slowly began to learn that a hammer is not the only tool available. I needed compassion and support from others, along with curiosity and critical inquiry. With patience and mindfulness, I have endeavored to get to the realities of my addiction and roots of the false beliefs I have had about myself, allowing layers of beliefs and energy to be peeled away and knots to be continually unraveled over the years. According to contemporary Buddhist meditation teacher Thanissara,

> As the awakening process integrates into our life, we are not lifted up and out of our challenges; instead it takes us down and through the layers of our personal and collective unconscious. As we become more aware, what is held in the shadow is illuminated. Inevitably we meet wounds related to themes of belonging, acceptance, safety, self-love, and self-expression.[17]

It might be helpful to think of a journey of transformative change as something done with baby steps. Ayurvedic doctor Vasant Lad has said that to un-do an addiction, for example, one should reduce the substance by 1/64th on a good day.[18] Using all of the healing justice capabilities—mindfulness, compassion, curiosity, critical inquiry, effort, and equanimity—one can bring awareness and energy to any form of unwholesome self-soothing that is causing unnecessary harm. Cold turkey does not work for most people as a sustainable way to change patterns, though sometimes it is necessary in the cases of lethal addictions. If one wants to quit smoking, which one may use to soothe nervous energy, cover up other negative feelings, or get a little energy lift, then one needs to be skillful as to how one goes about it. If one is feeling good that day, according to Lad's method, perhaps just smoking one less cigarette is a starting point. It can be a hard thing to take only baby steps when living in a culture of magic pills and quick fixes. If one is feeling out of sorts though, trying to make big changes too quickly may be experienced as a form of deprivation or violence and will not have the kind of effect that one would hope for; indeed, it could backfire. So discernment about what is the skillful and compassionate thing to do for oneself in any given moment is an essential element of a mindful approach to healing justice. The late Indian yoga teacher Swami Kripalu said, "Growth can only be gradual. The seed that is sown today does not sprout into a tree the next day. It does so only in the course of time, at its own pace, and by its own order."

Zen Buddhist teacher Joan Sutherland, who suffered from neurological and immunological problems for many years, referred to the experience of healing "not as the elimination of disease but as the falling in love with the poignancy of being alive."[19] While painful experiences are certainly ones that humans are naturally inclined to avoid, healing and transformation necessarily entail coming to terms with physical pain and dark emotions, and perhaps seeing the beauty of human pathos in the process. Sutherland goes on to write: "I came to see that my illness was a tear in the fabric of not just my life but in life-as-a-whole, and that my relations—human, spirit, plant, animal—were more than willing to help stitch it back up."[20] To be sure, in order to truly see ourselves as we are, heal, and find a more authentic self requires the mirror and support of others and the world around us.

Cultivating Balance

I have always been a person who is drawn to extreme experiences. I have been prone to immoderate indulgence in sensory pleasures, such as excessive amounts of food or intoxicants at one end of the spectrum and the austerities of spiritual practices, like waking up before dawn for extended periods of time to meditate or do yoga for hours, at the other end. In school and work, I have tended toward overachievement and intensity (e.g., I graduated from college in three years). When I wanted to engage further in research about recovery from disasters, I found myself in Port-au-Prince, Haiti, a few weeks after the devastating earthquake of 2010, in the midst of utter devastation and standing near a mass grave of tens of thousands of victims and committing to taking on a community research project that was beyond my real capacities. Slowly, I have been learning that this extreme behavior has been a mask covering a false belief about who I really am (i.e., that perhaps I am not enough and so more is better or I am bad to the core and good acts will change that).

Modern Buddhism and yoga offer advice on this issue of extremes— don't cultivate too much apathy, but don't cultivate too much asceticism either. It's the Middle Way that Buddha realized after he had been depriving himself of food and sleep to try and achieve enlightenment. Completely emaciated from his austerities, a milkmaid came by and offered him rice gruel to eat, and through this loving and compassionate act, he nourished himself with the food and came to realize that extreme asceticism was not working for him. This story has been interpreted as advice on the balance between masculine (discipline) and feminine (compassion) energies for our healing and transformation.[21]

Through my own healing journey I have tried many paths that have not worked—too much intense yoga, extreme exercise, and deprivation of many varieties and flavors—depriving myself of food, human connection, entertainment. These voices that goad one toward deprivation can be very sneaky and insidious, as their directions are often commensurate with ideas and images in the culture about what makes a good, happy, beautiful, or enlightened person (detox or cleanse, anyone?). For me, having been strongly influenced by spiritual practices that were originated by ascetics, it has been easy for me to rationalize the importance of engaging in extreme austerities to make changes in my life. Thankfully, I began to learn that healing and transformation are not about willpower but about allowing and creating the space for life to unfold. In my experience, it requires attention to the whole self, self-inquiry, and self-love. While discipline and sacrifice are definitely an important part of a healing journey (more on this later), one must balance this with compassion and the ability to let go in order to find both sustainability and true healing. Patanjali's *Yoga Sutras* echoes this as the author affirms the importance of embracing both *shtira*, making the right effort and trying one's best, and *sukka*, a sense of ease, sweetness, and repose.[22]

Of further significance on this journey is the cultivation of balance between self and the world. In human services and social change work, one might think of it as balancing one's social practice with one's own self-care; or balancing giving to others with giving to oneself. This requires discernment of the needs of the whole self in the unique contexts one finds oneself in, in order to understand more clearly when to set boundaries and when to be more expansive or generous with people. A physical practice like yoga can remind one that balance is a moving target that changes day to day and moment to moment. Moreover, one may find through personal inquiries that they tend to be more inclined toward one end of the spectrum or the other (self-care versus other-care), requiring one to perhaps get outside of the comfort zones of habitual patterning in that regard too. Clearly, it is a privilege to get to set such boundaries, and, depending on your social location and life circumstances, you may find that you have more or less capability or time to do it.

Digital Technology and Healing Justice

Living in an information age, it is especially apparent that humans love to get new information constantly. The human brain has actually evolved to seek out new information, which helped ancestors to be interested in seeking out new food sources and mates. What is not altogether clear, though, is whether all of this information is making modern humans any wiser or translating into better choices in terms of public policymaking, the health of the planet, or the choices each person makes in his or her own life. While access to information is a wonderful thing, my experience with technology is that it can be overwhelming and can take me away from my commitments to healing justice.

Sometimes I can feel like having a smartphone at my fingertips is a burden, just another addiction to try and overcome. It becomes a problem for me when I find myself mindlessly browsing or using it to "check out" of a situation that I need to be connected to. For example, I may find myself looking at e-mail during a meeting or checking for messages when I feel stuck on a work project. For me, the inquiry becomes: What am I trying to avoid? What am I really searching for? What void am I trying to fill? What am I in relationship to right now?

Of course, these technologies can make one feel more powerful as one coordinates efforts for a social action event through texting or Skypes on the phone with colleagues across the globe to enhance solidarity related to transnational projects. The point, at the end of the day, is to engage in an inquiry about what one's intentions, needs, and choices are in relation to one's use of technology. Like everything else in our lives, experiences with digital technology are grist for the mill for learning about ourselves and the world we live in, inviting us to take empowered action for healing and justice, moment to moment. You will notice throughout the book some inquiries and experiments for you to engage with that may help you culti-vate a more empowered relationship with technology.

The Six Capabilities in Balance

Some of the skills for change articulated in the previous section, including the cultivation of balance, can be fortified by going more deeply into the six capabilities that were introduced in the previous chapter. Thus, I discuss the three continua that were presented in the diagram in Chapter 3: mind-fulness and compassion, curiosity and critical inquiry, and effort and equa-nimity. At some level each capability represents the end of a continuum; on the other hand, they are intertwined, necessary for each other, and per-haps not as distinct as at first glance.

Mindfulness and Compassion

Mindfulness and compassion are the practices of being present and notic-ing what is happening in a nonjudgmental way. Mindfulness has three dimensions—awareness of what is happening, attention/focus/concen-tration, and remembering one's intention to be aware and attentive.[23] Thus mindfulness means accepting what is happening without judgment but with a quality of kindheartedness. Developing this kind of relation-ship with oneself requires one to slow down, relax, bring one's attention inward, and tune in. Because one's attention is often focused outside of oneself (e.g., what's on the screen, what someone else might be think-ing, or what is going to happen in the future), the skill of turning inward can be a challenging one to cultivate and may actually be contraindicated for those who are overwhelmed by unresolved trauma. Outwardly focused attention may be especially common for those who have been victims of violence or if their own or their children's survival depends on being vigilant in relation to systemic violence, such as police brutality. But even a little bit of mindfulness can offer tools for many people to reclaim their attention and personal power. Mindfulness practice may be of the formal variety (e.g., sitting quietly for a set period of time alone or with a group of people) or informal (e.g., while doing the dishes or standing in line).

Formal mindfulness practices have been studied extensively especially in the past 10 years, and there are literally hundreds of studies from the fields of medicine, psychology, social work, education, and other fields on the effectiveness of mindfulness meditation with a range of populations for a host of conditions, including the general population.[24–26] For instance, there is significant empirical evidence on the effectiveness of mindfulness-based stress reduction (MBSR), an eight-week program of guided instruction in mindfulness and mindful body movement. MBSR has been shown to have positive impact on brain function, immune activity, chronic pain, stress, caregiver stress, disordered eating, and cancer.[27] While I discuss more of these studies in greater detail in Part II as I flesh out the actual practices, it is worth noting here that there is also evidence that formal mindfulness practice can have negative outcomes for some people.

One dimension of mindfulness that was introduced in the previous chapter is interoception, which is an internal awareness of one's body and specifically sensations such as tightness, openness, hunger, thirst, temperature, and muscular sensations. Of course, humans naturally have this capability, but the prefrontal cortex of the brain can shift one's attention away from these sensations and cognition can convince one to override bodily needs. And, as noted before, the current cultural milieu encourages disconnection from ourselves and has perhaps diminished our capabilities for mindfulness. What is interesting about this kind of perception in the body is that it is wholly subjective and can have a kind of muddiness or mysteriousness to it. Feeling into one's body and knowing something is wrong is a different kind of knowing than what a blood test, for example, would provide. There is an infinite horizon to the edges of such perception, which is part of the reason it can be such a beautiful practice and a poetic antidote to a world of sharp edges, firm deadlines, spreadsheets, computer bytes, and PIN numbers.[28] It does take time to stop and notice, and it takes commitment to stay with the practice and to develop these skills, but eventually the practices can become so ingrained that there is a more natural alignment with one's internal landscape or, as the yogis say, a yoking. Mind-body practices such as hatha yoga, Feldenkrais, somatic experiencing, and tai chi are examples of other disciplines or interventions that can help a person to develop these skills.

To be sure, in popular culture, mindfulness has arguably become another commodity in the neoliberal marketplace of self-care remedies being sold as something that can improve corporations, the military, and schools, creating a phenomenon that has been referred to as McMindfulness. From a healing justice perspective, though, mindfulness itself can be reclaimed, as well as be thought of as an act of resistance to disconnection, marginalization, and internalized oppression. And, to be very clear, I am not arguing that mindfulness is a Trojan horse that will magically change organizations, systems, political parties, the economy, or culture. Such changes can only come through organizing, mobilization, direct action, and resistance. It should be clear that I am arguing that we need to do both kinds of work—internal and external.

A necessary companion to mindfulness is compassion. In the Buddhist tradition, compassion is for "all beings, *including oneself*."[29] According to the Dalai Lama,

> for someone to develop genuine compassion towards others, first he or she must have a basis upon which to cultivate compassion, and that basis is the ability to connect one's own feelings and to care for one's own welfare. . . . Caring for others requires caring for oneself.[30]

A meditation student once asked the Dalai Lama about how to deal with low self-esteem. He and his interpreter were confused by the question as they realized that there are no words in the Tibetan language that captures the idea of low self-esteem. So one could say that low self-esteem is culturally constructed, as many people have internalized a cultural propensity toward judgment and self-judgment. This is part of the reason that self-compassion can be so difficult for many people to cultivate.

It is fairly common for practitioners, and perhaps most people, to have more compassion for others and less compassion for themselves, criticizing and judging any thought, feeling, or behavior that is less than one's ideal of perfection. Others may be more inclined to point the finger at others, blaming and critiquing them, while leaving themselves off the hook. So you may find that you have to work on cultivating one more than the other. Ultimately, though, cultivating compassion for self and others is a synergistic process, one that is connected to the ability to be mindful.

Indeed, research has shown that practices such as mindfulness meditation and yoga can result in higher levels of both self-compassion and empathy, which are all related to higher levels of psychological functioning. One study found that various dimensions of empathy, such as perspective taking, are associated with mindfulness.[31] One's levels of self-compassion appear to play an important role in one's ability to take on the perspective of another, clearly a critical skill for counselors and human services workers. Research reveals that high levels of self-compassion are associated with greater levels of emotional well-being, physical health, and interpersonal functioning[32] and that self-compassion exercises have been shown to have positive effects on the functioning and well-being of therapists.[33]

In the end, the process of developing self-compassion and empathy can expand the field for what is possible in one's life in unfathomable ways. Meditation teacher Sharon Salzberg writes,

> The division between self and other is the degradation of one's highest human potential: the liberation of the mind that is love. The critical moment of the path, which breaks open the loving heart, is the realization that we have never existed as separate, isolated beings. When wisdom recognizes our oneness and sees the interconnectedness of all beings, it fills us with a degree of happiness that transforms our lives.[34]

Thus this kind of radical self-care may be thought of as planting the seeds for revolutionizing the world and dissolving the false divides that perpetuate war, injustice, poverty, and other forms of violence. While most people are conditioned to think that they possess only finite quantities of love and compassion, consider the possibility that it is an infinite resource that gives endlessly and is always available to everyone. For the practices to work for one's own and others' healing and transformation, one's compassion and self-compassion must be indefatigable and relentless.

Curiosity and Critical Inquiry

At some level, healing justice practice invites practitioners to take an interest in their lives in the way an investigator or scientist might, as one takes a step back and places a wedge between one's experience and the one who observes that experience in order to gain some perspective. To be clear, though, the curiosity needed here is a curiosity of the heart; it is not an intellectual curiosity. According to meditation teacher Rodney Smith, "There is a primary curiosity of the heart that is the force of life attempting to complete itself. In its purest form, primary curiosity transforms all expressions of ignorance into truth."[35] Curiosity has an open quality to it and does not have expectations, hopes, or wishes for the outcome of the investigation. Of course, we are human and we do have desires for ourselves, as well as beliefs that can lurk below the surface, so part of the practice is to bring those into awareness too.

Curiosity requires some intentionality because people are so prone to judging themselves and they have so much at stake. So curiosity's close friends are compassion and equanimity. Even when people realize that they are engaged in patterning or behavior that they would like to change, oftentimes the best course of action is to do nothing about it, particularly when first starting out on the healing journey. Over time, one can go deeper into the inquiry, to learn about the causes and conditions that tend to make the behavior arise. For example, every time a certain colleague talks at a faculty meeting, I find myself prone to checking out. Perhaps it begins with an internal (or external) eye roll on my part, followed by an internal dialogue that judges the person. This is followed by a thought stream filled with ways to respond to her that will rebut or contradict what she is saying (even though I am not actually listening very well to what she is saying in the first place). All of this can happen in just a few short seconds. Moreover, it appears to be deeply conditioned in my system and likely originated far before I even came to know this person. It can be very difficult to bring it into awareness and to get enough perspective on it to be able to investigate it. But, sometimes and certainly not always, an attitude of curiosity graces me and invites me to ask questions—What's going on here? What is this really about? What are the power dynamics here? Is this pattern serving my own, her's, and others' highest good? As Swami Kripalu said, "The highest spiritual practice is self-observation with love."

Critical inquiry is a counterpart to curiosity and is essential because it invites people into a dialectical conversation between their habitual patterning and their environment. In Sanskrit, the word *viveka*, or discernment is relevant, as an acumen or keen perception that can help people distinguish what is skillful or unskillful or wholesome or unwholesome for them in any given moment. It is a conscious engagement with the cognitive dimension of the self. This capability can help individuals to understand the ways that their experiences with oppression, for example, can bind them, separating them from their power, and challenge them to bring forth something different. It provides a tool to ask themselves whether in any given moment they are standing in their own power or giving up power to someone or something else. Drawing from Karpman's drama triangle, they can inquire into whether in some relational situation one might be unconsciously playing the perpetrator, rescuer or victim, and how that might be prefigured by past experiences.[36] Noticing this, they can learn about themselves and their conditioning and make more empowered decisions in terms of actions and behaviors.

Foucault argued that power over others in society, or biopower, is exercised through various means but particularly by means of social discourses and the practices of institutions.[37] Whether it is the surveillance practices of the criminal justice system or the ways in which schools silence the voices of children, these mechanisms can serve to create docile bodies, which are crippled in their ability to understand injustice and to effect change in the world. His attention to the body is especially relevant to the work of healing justice, which is concerned with disentangling oppression and disempowerment in the whole self. With the skills of mindfulness, compassion, and curiosity, in solidarity with one's colleagues, people can use their capabilities for critical thinking and discernment to unpack the mechanisms of oppression that manifest in organizations, communities, and themselves.

Bringing critical inquiry into healing justice practice furthers the capability to make the practices transformative. Individuals can inquire into the means by which culture, economic systems, and social institutions contribute to a situation or any kind of stickiness they finds themselves in. Relatedly, people can look at the ways that their experiences with their family of origin and ancestors may contribute to thought or behavioral patterns. Critical inquiry is especially important because if people overemphasize their capabilities for compassion at the expense of critical thinking, they can find themselves in vulnerable positions, perhaps being manipulated by others more powerful than them. It can also cause them to lose perspective on social injustice and the subtle ways that unchecked power hurts people in innumerable ways.

Effort and Equanimity

In the classical teachings of yoga, there are two concepts that are helpful when considering undertaking the practices—*abhyasa*, which is the determined effort of regular, committed practice, and *vairagya*, renunciation of the fruits of practice, also called equanimity. When discussing *abhyasa*, or effort, Patanjali states, "Practice becomes firmly grounded when well attended to for a long time, without break and in all earnestness."[38] This is the kind of *effort* needed so that the practices offered in this book can heal and transform. Accordingly, establishing healing justice as a practice necessitates the creation of a certain amount of structure. Such structure may include setting the intention to engage in a practice for a certain amount of time or number of repetitions, like starting a session before one meets with a client with five deep breaths, or renouncing something, such as setting the intention not to look at one's cell phone for an hour before bed. Within this kind of structure of one's own choosing, one may find that it is not confining or restricting of one's sense of freedom at all. Perhaps one may find a richer kind of freedom much different than what one normally thinks of as freedom, namely the freedom to do whatever one wants.

The nature of effort is that it must be renewed; one must commit and recommit to one's intention to heal and transform until it becomes effortless. Most people (including myself) can relate to trying to start a new routine or habit, only to fall off the wagon after an embarrassingly short period of time. Re-committing efforts is especially important if one is just starting out on a path of healing justice as practice. It may necessitate setting intentions to practice regularly and becoming willing to hold oneself, one's colleagues, and one's comrades on the path, accountable. Renewing efforts may mean letting go of clinging to the inner, whining adolescent who does not want to get out of bed in the morning, or to the harried adult that claims to be too busy and stressed out to slow down and reconnect. As the practices become more firmly rooted in one's internal system, it becomes easier to ignore the inner whiner and harried adult and to sustain the practices, guided by an authentic wisdom. Persistence is clearly one of the key sources for sustaining healing justice practice. When I asked one of my Zen teachers once about what the secret to meditation practice was, he leaned toward me and softly whispered, "Don't stop."

One's commitment to making an effort will only be successful when it is balanced with the other capabilities—equanimity, mindfulness, compassion, curiosity, and critical inquiry. If one fixates too much on effort, there will be diminishing returns, and ultimately one's efforts will be sabotaged. Geneen Roth, author of *Women, Food and God,* says that change does not happen by depriving yourself; it happens through loving yourself.

Thus the counterpart to effort is equanimity or *vairagya*, also trans-
lated as renunciation. I also like to think of it as "letting go." Equanimity
can be understood as acceptance of things as they are. This capability is
also an important companion to mindfulness. Psychologist and meditation teacher Tara Brach calls it radical acceptance, which she says "is the
gateway to healing wounds and spiritual transformation. When we can
meet our experience with Radical Acceptance, we discover the wholeness,
wisdom and love that are our deepest nature."[39] Similarly, one of the contemporary mindfulness-based psychotherapeutic interventions, known as
Acceptance and Commitment Therapy, makes acceptance of problems,
thoughts, and struggles central to the intervention. As humanist psychologist Carl Rogers wrote, "The curious paradox is that when I accept myself
just as I am, then I can change." The same is true of one's outer social justice and human services work. We have to see the problems and strengths
in the situation exactly as they are before we can take effective action.

It is tempting to think of equanimity as purely a quality of the mind,
the ability to be calm and cool in difficult situations. This is an important
dimension of this virtue. But I find that cultivating equanimity is also an
embodied experience, connected to my ability to relax. One can cultivate
this skill when one encounters tension or unsettling energy in the body
by bringing kind awareness and acceptance to it, by exhaling deeply, or by
consciously and gently releasing any sense of gripping or tightness, allowing one to potentially settle into the fullness of the experience. This process can deepen equanimity. Moreover, this applies to any kind of practice
that one is engaged in, whether one is facilitating a group in the community, taking care of children, or walking in the park mindfully. Equanimity
means that one doesn't take everything so personally. One can allow the
moment to unfold with a sense of calm and ease, not trying to change it
or add anything to it.

Another dimension to the meaning of *vairagya* is concerned with
withdrawal from the material world into the spiritual, a call to renounce
worldly things. Though the purpose in this modern context is not for
practitioners to become monastics or to transcend earthly concerns, it can
often be helpful to renounce "worldly" things on occasion as a part of a
healing practice—whether it is giving up chocolate for Lent, or having a
technology fast one day a week, or going on a silent meditation retreat for a
weekend. One has to be careful though with renunciation because one can
go too far with it, or it can be contraindicated for some people. Perhaps the
baby steps discussed earlier in the chapter are a more appropriate route; it

all depends on the person and situation. To be sure, the purpose of such renunciation is not to deprive oneself of pleasure, which will certainly just result in the perpetuation of a sense of scarcity, disconnecting one from their heart and the hearts of others. Ultimately, when one renounces wisely, it can free up energy and allow one to foster connections to previously unknown dimensions of the self, others, and environment.

There is yet one other aspect to this yogic concept of *vairagya*. It is the idea of letting go, especially of the expectations that one may have for their healing practice. Very often, I find that I have subtle expectations about my meditation, such as hoping that it will calm me down when I'm feeling agitated, release tension in my neck, cause me to become enlightened someday soon, or make me into a heroic person that everyone will love and admire. For a time, I also thought, though I would never have admitted it to anyone, that practicing yoga would help me to get a "perfect" body. When practices don't result in these unspoken hopes, one can become frustrated and give up. While it is certainly appropriate to have goals, intentions, and hopes, it is important to inquire into whether one might be dwelling in an unrealistic or delusional fantasy and/or trying to control what happens. In the end, the invitation is to do these practices with great vigor and gusto, while simultaneously being humble enough to let go of what the outcome might be.

Nurturing the Positive

In order to stay the path, people have to feel like they are getting something important and meaningful from the healing justice practices, that they are surely impacting their personal and professional life. As you begin to explore and benefit from the transformative practices offered here, you may find yourself wanting to do more of them. If that is the case, then there is a positive feedback loop at work. As you start out, though, it is helpful to come from a place where there is more positive in your life than negative, or else the negative may overwhelm you and you may be less inclined to do the practices, perhaps slipping into unwholesome habitual patterns that are all too familiar or just getting comfortable with the status quo. Thus to cultivate a field for the whole self that is nourishing and pleasant, it is useful to create a container that can hold all of the paradoxes of one's life and work. This is what the drumming did for Jacky. Another way to do this is to learn to nurture the positive.

The practice, known as "nurturing the positive," "taking in the good," or "hardwiring happiness," is an evidence-based intervention, grounded in mindfulness practice and developed by a neuropsychologist to help people experience more positivity in their life.[40] The practice takes advantage of the power of self-directed, experience-dependent neuroplasticity such that the brain can actually change and help one to overcome a tendency toward negativity. The idea behind it is that, by doing the practices, one can "*activate* mental states and then *install* them as neural traits."[41]

There are clearly wonderful benefits to nurturing the positive, whether it is the development of a more positive outlook or perspective, pleasant feelings or sensations, or appreciating positive experiences. Happiness has been conceptualized as being engaged in the world, being in the "flow," and having a sense of meaning in life.[42] It is associated with greater resilience, and some research has shown that people who are happy and/or optimistic actually tend to be healthier and to live longer than those who are pessimistic.[43] Other research has shown associations between happiness and altruistic behavior.[44] If people could cultivate more happiness in their lives, surely it would help them to be more resilient and effective change makers. It is also important to remember that the purpose of this practice is not to pretend that one is happy when one is not, or to push away difficult emotions or experiences. It is not a program in new age "power of positive thinking." It is simply a practice to consciously cultivate a more spacious container for holding the challenges of one's life and work.

One way to nurture the positive in daily life is to savor and prolong pleasurable experiences. Clinical psychologist Charles Styron[45] suggests several ways to do this: sharing a positive experience one has with others, building and storing memories and images, self-congratulation, sharpening and articulating, and absorption. Individuals can intensify pleasurable experiences using the practice of mindfulness, bringing their attention to what is happening and the sensations and feelings the experience is evoking. Hanson teaches that people can notice a positive experience they are having and then deepen it by marinating in the pleasurable sensations and absorbing it into their system.[46] This practice of "taking it in" can apply to a wide range of daily experiences. For example, you can allow yourself time to pause after an interaction with a client or colleague that was socially productive (known as compassion satisfaction), taking in the satisfaction or pleasures into your system, and even congratulating yourself for a job well done. When you feel a warm breeze outside after a long winter, allow the pleasure of the experience to marinate in your system, taking a few breaths and leaning into it. You can do this throughout your day, coming back to the practice regularly until you find that perhaps the practices start to "do you."

In the end, healing justice practice is about learning to be with the fullness of the human experience, much of which one usually tends to be unaware of, or tries to avoid. The goal is not for every experience that one has to be happy and positive. Life is not like that, and the so-called negative experiences, or "shadow" part of the self, actually serve a purpose. One can learn to be with the shadow side experiences and allow them to help one grow, or serve as a wake-up call for change. But, because of the negativity bias (i.e., that brains are wired to be "Teflon for the good and Velcro for the bad"), the practice of taking in the good can help one to overcome it.[47] Eventually, one can use this practice strategically, as a foundation for the capabilities of mindfulness and compassion, effort and equanimity, and curiosity and critical inquiry, thereby enhancing one's potential for healing.

Putting It Into Practice
Inquiry

Reflect on your typical weekday routine and consider a time of day when you would like to be more present, more aware of what is going on internally and externally. This is a time of day or activity when you tend to experience the most stress. Examples may include when you are getting ready in the morning, driving in traffic, meeting with a supervisor, at the beginning, middle, or end of certain meetings, completing paperwork at your job, or transitioning from work to home. Choose one challenging time/activity and write it on top of a piece of paper. Take several days to engage in an inquiry about that activity each time you do it. Consider the following questions as you journal about it or reflect on it with someone: How do you feel in your body and mind when you are doing it? What are the causes and conditions that lead up to any discomfort you experience with the activity? Do you have any knowledge about how people in your life have handled this activity, currently or in the past—your caregivers, teachers, partner, colleagues? Do you notice any underlying beliefs, wishes, or fears about this time/activity? How might the larger culture/economy/social systems influence your relationship with this time/activity? Notice any other insights that might be present. The purpose here is not necessarily to change anything but to learn about your whole self by being mindful of what's happening in conjunction with your capabilities for compassion, curiosity, and critical inquiry. A particular inclination toward some sort of counter-action may naturally arise after engaging in this inquiry (e.g., deciding to slow down when cooking dinner after having noticed that it is something you rush through), but it is your choice whether to make any changes or to just let the wisdom you might have gained be for now.

Self-Care Practice Skill

Find a comfortable place to lie down flat on your back. The floor is ideal (on a rug or yoga mat), but a firm couch or bed will work too. Bring both of your legs and arms straight into the air. (Make any modifications for your body that are appropriate, e.g. if you are not able to use your legs, then just raise your arms, or vice versa). Some people call this "dead bug pose." Begin to shake out all four limbs. This can be done as gently and slowly or as rapidly and vigorously as feels right for you. Try to do it for a minute or more if you can, taking deep breaths as you do it. When you are done, bring your arms and legs back down to the floor and close your eyes. Turn your awareness inside and notice what sensations you feel. Tune into any positivity that is present, a sense of calm, flow, or relaxed sensations. Allow it to be a wordless experience where you are just feeling. Stay with the experience for a few minutes, allowing any positive feeling from it to marinate and absorb into your system. If you find it to be a largely negative experience, just notice that without judging.

Experiment for a Day

For one day, you will do a basic practice of "taking in the good" or "nurturing the positive." Your experiment is to notice any good experiences throughout your day—a pleasant sound such as birds chirping or music playing, a shared joke with a friend, a tasty treat, or a loving connection with a pet, child, or partner. The practice is simply to notice the experiences and let them nourish you, locking in the different dimensions of the experience—in the body, emotions, or thoughts. Let the experiences soak into your system and truly enjoy them for yourself; practice doing this with equanimity and nonattachment to outcomes.